Updated Second Edition

Women Make Great Entrepreneurs.

Here's Why. Here's How.

Jane.
Success!
As YOU want it.
David B-J
3/99

David Bryn-Jones

Learn How To Start Your Own Business

Women Make Great Entrepreneurs

Here's Why. Here's How.

David Bryn-Jones
Updated Second Edition

Published by GreenBank Books.
Phone: 250-537-2097 Fax: 250-537-2095
e-mail: brynjones@saltspring.com web: www.islandnet.com/brynjones
132 Bullock Creek Road, Salt Spring Island, BC, Canada V8K 2L3
and 180 - 145 Tyee Drive, Point Roberts, WA 98281

Editing: Christine McBeath
Cover Design: Colin Campbell
Book Design: Robb Zuk

Library of Congress No. 97-67677

C.C.I.P. Data

Bryn-Jones, David, 1931 -
Women Make Great Entrepreneurs. Here's Why. Here's How.

ISBN 0-9683388-0-1

1. Businesswomen. 2. Entrepreneurship. 3. Women-owned business enterprises.
4. New business enterprises. I. Title.

HD6072.5.B79 1998 650.1'082 C98-900208-X

1998 1999 2000 2001 2002 / 10 9 8 7 6 5 4 3 2

Dedication

To my grandchildren, for whose benefit this book is written.

Alexander

Arlo

Owen

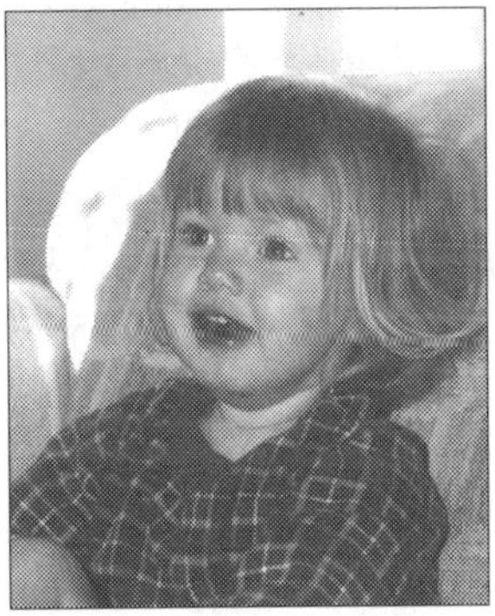

Hannah

Helena

Acknowledgements

I'd like to thank friends, family and colleagues for help and encouragement with this book:

Susan Janet Biddlecombe, *my wife*

Alice Acheson
Cheryl Bailey
Erin, Michael Biddlecombe
Megan, Evan, Laura, Gail Bryn-Jones
Colin Campbell
Diana Douglas
Diana English
Dianne Fidler
David Galway
Mary Halpen
Lorraine Harvey
Johanna Hoskins
Maggie Kerrigan
Mary Kirner
Paul Marcano
Christine McBeath
Kelly McCallum
Shari Macdonald
Robert Mackwood
Lisa Persson
Katherine Plett
Linda Kavelin Popov
Suzanne Prendergast
Carolyn Prentice
Ralph Prentice
Norma Smith
Martin Thorn
Evelyn Valcourt
Kate Walker
Julie Weeks
Helen Werry
Robb Zuk

...and on the cover — top to bottom, left to right:

Marty Postlethwait	p. 25
Best of Bridge partners	p. 29
Marla Stritzel Sloan	p. 27
Margaret Huszar	p. 138
Monique Maddy	p. 30
Barbara Slater	p. 130
Chris Czajkowski	p. 90

It is in the shelter of each other that people live. – Irish Proverb

Contents

Woman's Creed

Wise Women
Strong Women
Life-giving Women
Women of Spirit
Women of Power
Women of Peace
Blessed Be

– Unknown

Women Do Make Great Entrepreneurs
YOU Can Be One
Our Planet Welcomes You
Our Planet Needs You.

– David Bryn-Jones

Prologue

Two convictions drive me. Our planet will be safer and kinder when women have more to do with managing it. Being an entrepreneur is the highest business calling.

Like all grandchildren, my five are exceptional: bright, beautiful, destined to be positive contributors to their world. But what is their world- and that of their grandchildren- going to be like over the next 50 to 100 years?

At the moment, we humans are systematically wounding our environment, its resources and its species. Do you know that there are only some 3,000 of the magnificent Bengal tigers left on earth? And according to a digital readout on the Bronx Zoo's Jungle World: Every minute we cut and burn 100 more acres of tropical rain forest.

As a citizen, I'm sad about environmental deterioration. As a man, I'm embarrassed. As a parent, I'm guilty because I've paid so little attention.

But happily, reality checks often set the stage for positive ideas and action. As "Daido" (Welsh for Grandpa) to five gorgeous young humans, I wish to contribute towards improving the health of the world they will inherit. Hence this book.

The book is directed primarily at ambitious, intelligent and conscientious women. The message is also valid for ambitious, intelligent and conscientious men.

The world now needs compassionate, more socially responsible management. In my opinion, the world will more likely receive such management from powerful, senior women, than from powerful, senior men. To be in positions that influence humanitarian work on the scale visualized, women will need world-wide political and financial power. This power is developing as a result of the rapid growth of women entrepreneurs.

I suggest that women are naturally predisposed to the nurturing attitudes that will encourage humanitarian investment, management and work. With a willingness for conciliation and adjustment, they know that contemporary management involves listening and sharing. Women place importance on relationships, and criteria for success in business among women entrepreneurs often extend beyond the monetary.

From the evidence (see examples in this book) many senior women entrepreneurs, after attaining personal business success, begin to blend financial and business goals with charitable activities. Their inclination for "giving back" to their communities through charitable activities is dramatic — 78% vs 48% of all adults.

I contend therefore that, acting *collectively*, women entrepreneurs could represent enormous potential financial, political and cultural power. These focused and successful women entrepreneurs would offer huge hope for environmental and humanitarian work.

I am *not* placing the burden of "saving the world" entirely on women entrepreneurs, but I do believe that women entrepreneurs will more likely adopt socially sensitive management practices, and that they will set positive examples.

Nor am I suggesting that the new woman entrepreneur will have the time or the inclination to consider local or global issues. She will be busy enough balancing her own needs with those of her family and her business. Possibly though, she will observe the involvement of her senior peers and include some similar objectives among her goals.

I simply hope to increase awareness among both successful and aspiring women entrepreneurs of the colossal potential power in their hands.

In whatever way 78% of women entrepreneurs choose to give back to their community, the world will be the beneficiary.

Therefore the more of them there are doing so, the better!

It is a privilege to include in my book inspiring role model stories received from women entrepreneurs all over North America. Encouraging other women to emulate these entrepreneurs is the essence of this book.

The final chapter contains my dream for developing new care for the world of my grandchildren. The chapter immediately preceding introduces the story of one woman's majestic global mission, a vision which gives me hope for mine.

On behalf of grandchildren everywhere, I challenge you to dream *your* dream, and to pursue it.

David Bryn-Jones
Salt Spring Island

July 1998

A woman's place is in the world.

– Unknown

1

Women Make Great Entrepreneurs. You Can Be One!

You can be one of the millions of women entrepreneurs in North America.

As of 1996, there were nearly 8 million women-owned businesses in the US; nearly 900,000 in Canada.[1]

Women become entrepreneurs for many reasons. Some are frustrated by barriers to career advancement. Some want a particular work culture or flexibility they cannot find in conventional jobs. Over forty percent of women business owners said they started their businesses with an idea for a product or service, or a feeling that they could do for themselves what they did for an employer. There's the obvious lure of a higher income. Perhaps real wealth. There's the chance for prestige, esteem in the eyes of peers, associates and family. This can lead to greater things too: politics perhaps, high appointments in charities, business honors etc. Down deep, women probably want to succeed as entrepreneurs to prove many things to themselves.

Why are women great entrepreneurs?

It is the usually conservative approach and the enormous commitment a woman makes that helps produce her success. The entrepreneurial woman is probably embarking on a new way of life, perhaps for basic survival. It is not just a career change.

---

1 All of the information in this chapter about women entrepreneurs in the US and Canada has come from the following:

a) *Women-Owned Businesses in the United States: A Fact Sheet, 1996—The National Foundation For Women Business Owners.* For information about individual state fact sheets or other available publications about women-owned businesses, contact the National Foundation for Women Business Owners at: 830-1100 Wayne Avenue, Silver Springs, MD 20910-5603.

b) *The Economic Power of Women-led Firms in Canada,* a study similar to the NFWBO study, highlights the facts set out above. Contact Bank of Montreal's Institute for Small Business, 3550 Pharmacy Avenue, Scarborough, Ontario, Canada M1W 3Z3.

c) Statistics Canada.

Women entrepreneurs succeed because they:

- thoroughly study the business they are considering, often taking a long time to do so
- are likely to listen to wisdom advising them to write and use a business plan
- are patient and realistic about the time and effort required to get their businesses going
- are likely to seek and accept professional guidance, attend business courses and seminars
- accept a lower income from their businesses initially, with less need for trappings of success
- in changing their basic way of life by going into business, women seem open to new ideas, and willing to persevere when the going gets tough.

- **Women business owners demonstrate their own "styles of success," showing in both word and deed that their ways of management and leadership are distinctly different from their male counterparts.**

  Women business owners are more likely to emphasize intuitive thinking, stressing creativity, sensitivity and values. Men business owners are more likely to emphasize logical thinking, stressing analysis, processing information methodically and developing procedures.

  Women business owners' thinking styles are more evenly balanced between logic and intuition so they are more easily able to switch among multiple tasks. Further, since they place value on both relationships and facts, women are more likely to seek out the opinions of others.

  Women business owners are more reflective when making decisions, weighing outcomes before acting, gathering more information and advice prior to rendering a decision.

  Women do manage differently, as shown by the employee benefits they offer in the US:

  - Women are likely to provide the same level of basic employee benefits as all small businesses—including health care, paid vacation and personal leave.
  - Plus, they are more likely to offer such additional benefits as flex-time and tuition reimbursements, and, at a much smaller size, to share profits with employees.

In times of change, learners inherit the earth

– Unknown

- Further, among firms with 10 or more employees that do not have a retirement plan, women business owners are discussing the issue of retirement more than men business owners, and a greater share of these women intend to implement a retirement plan soon.

- **Satisfactions from building relationships, "giving something back" and being in control of one's destiny, are all key rewards of entrepreneurship for women. Challenge still lies, however, in being taken seriously.**

  The greatest reward of entrepreneurship, according to women business owners is the empowerment they feel at controlling their own destiny.

  Women business owners also state that they derive great satisfaction through building relationships—with customers, employees and suppliers, and in giving something back to their communities.

  Fully 78% of women business owners spend time volunteering, compared to 48% of all adults in the US. They are also more likely to encourage their employees to volunteer.

  Half of these women volunteer for more than one charity, and having children appears to be a catalyst for a higher level of volunteer activity.

  The greatest challenge women business owners face, in their own words, is being taken seriously—proving their personal capability and the credibility of their business.

  Being taken seriously is a greater problem for women who own businesses in "non-traditional" industries—such as manufacturing, construction and transportation—and for older women business owners.

- **Women-owned firms are just as financially strong and creditworthy as the average firm. Further, there has been significant improvement in access to capital for women-owned businesses.**

  Based on three broad measures of financial strength tracked by Dun & Bradstreet—promptness of paying bills, credit risk and overall financial stress—women-owned firms show no significant difference from average US firms.

  Further analysis of these indices reveals that regardless of industry or size of firm, there is no significant difference in the financial strength and creditworthiness of women-owned firms and all US firms.

  There has been remarkable progress in access to capital for women-owned firms. Between 1992 and 1996, the share of women-owned firms using credit cards for short-term financing has dropped in half, while the share using business earnings has doubled.

Banking relationships have improved for women-business owners since 1992. At that time, nearly two of three women (65%) reported some difficulties in working with their bank; being denied financing due to limited collateral or assets, finding the credit process too complicated, or perceiving mistreatment owing to being a woman. Currently, over 50% of women business owners report no such difficulties.

- **Women business owners are taking a more proactive approach than men business owners in adopting new technology for growth; 23% of women-owned firms, compared to 16% of men-owned firms, have an Internet home page; 47% of women compared to 41% of men entrepreneurs subscribe to an on-line service.**

Both women and men business owners have plans for acquiring technology. What differentiates the use of technology is the industry, the size and age of the firm.

Studies indicate that women enjoy technology, using it confidently as a tool for advancement. Beepers, cell phones, computers, e-mail and the Internet etc give women access to fields often belonging to males and college educated women.

What is the result of this progress?

In the US

As of 1966, there are nearly eight million women-owned businesses in the US employing over 18.5 million and generating close to $2.3 trillion in sales. Nearly 1.1 million (13%) of the women-owned businesses in the US, employing nearly 1.7 million, and generating over $180 billion in sales, are owned by women of color.

In 1996, women-owned firms accounted for one-third (36%) of all the firms in the country, provided employment for one out of every four (26%) US workers and generated 16% of the nation's business sales.

Since 1990, the annual growth in businesses started by women has averaged over 350.000. The largest share of women-owned firms is in the service sector: 4 million (52%) in services; 1.5 million (19.5%) in retailing; 800,000 (10%) in finance, insurance or real estate; the remainder are in many other businesses.

- Women are diversifying into non-traditional businesses. The greatest growth in the number of women-owned firms is in: construction, wholesale trade, transportation, communications, agriculture and manufacturing.

- Women-owned firms have tenacity. They are more likely to have remained in business over the past three years than the average US firm, and the average age of women-owned businesses is approaching that of all US firms.

In Canada

As of 1997, there are more than 850,000 women-led firms in Canada, providing jobs for more than 1.7 million Canadians, and employing more people than the largest 100 Canadian companies combined.

- Between 1993 and 1996, the number of women-led firms grew at over 74,000 per year, twice the rate of all firms in Canada, and the rate of employment in women-led firms grew at four times the average rate.
- Women-led firms are as financially strong, as creditworthy, and as tenacious (76% survival rate, 1991 to 1994) as the average Canadian company.
- Nearly half (45.6%) of Canadian women-led businesses are in retailing. The remainder are spread through agriculture, mining, construction, manufacturing, wholesale, personal and business services.

What about you?

At a time when corporate North America is mega-merging or downsizing; moving production overseas; replacing labor with technology, temps and contractors; women entrepreneurs are starting businesses at about twice the rate of men. Women-owned firms will continue to grow as an enormous force in the North American and world economies—economically, culturally, socially, financially and politically.

> *An ounce of action is worth a ton of theory.* – F. Engels

Where will you be as this massive North American trend towards women's entrepreneurship and development of power continues? Will you be one of these entrepreneurs? You are the architect of your own destiny. There are no entitlements. You have to work at it. You will have to make choices. But you can be one of them. You **can be** one of the millions of successful women entrepreneurs in the world.

As women gain confidence from their accomplishments, become better trained and more independent, they understand that it is their innate natures which give them the strength to be leaders. A woman's company is like her family where she encourages, comforts, rewards and conciliates.

Women know they cannot do everything alone. They are willing to work with others, to modify, adjust and cooperate to achieve an end; to make a difference in business and in the lives of many people they touch.

Beginning with an honest self-analysis, moving through careful preparation and planning, developing essential family and other support systems, there is no reason why you can't enjoy a thriving business.

You can achieve more in the next five years than you ever thought possible, perhaps make a difference to the whole world.

> One by-product of the explosion of women entrepreneurs is the phenomenon of men staying at home to assume family responsibilities, to be the vital supportive spouse. These role reversals are not necessarily easy for men, but there are bonuses. There can be relief from careers in unfulfilling jobs, new opportunities to develop other interests, maybe home-based businesses of their own. Perhaps most importantly, there is the participation in the development of their children during ages often missed.

> *The best things in life aren't things.*
>
> – Unknown

2

Key Questions About Yourself

Good answers to strong questions will not, by themselves, define whether or not you'd make a good entrepreneur. Heart, soul, creativity, commitment, tenacity, persistence, desire, motivation, courage—these can't be measured by questions. But questions do force you to consider aspects of yourself and your personality that you may not normally be willing to assess.

If you are seriously thinking about becoming an entrepreneur, you are wise to answer the searching questions starting on page 185. Do so slowly, and mostly for your own benefit. Think honestly about the implications.

No quiz can accurately answer questions regarding your skills, ideas, toughness and dedication. These questions only get answered in the crucible of life.

Here are some of the broad questions many women entrepreneurs think through—or wish they had—before they set down the first line of their business plans:

How Do I Rate as a Potential Entrepreneur?

- **Is my idea good enough?**

  Few entrepreneurs would dispute the role a breakthrough idea plays in getting a company off the ground. Occasionally, there's a seminal idea that turns a casual inventor into a millionaire—Velcro, as an example. But mostly, an entrepreneur works hard to turn an improvement on an existing idea into something newly useful and exciting to others.

  The key question is will anyone actually buy what is offered?
- **Have I the management skills I need?**
  Ask yourself what you're good at. Then ask other people if they agree with your self-evaluation. You might be surprised.

  But you'll learn what you have to improve upon. Most entrepreneurs possess a mixture of skills, some specific to their project, others with broad applications to all businesses.

> *Make the most of yourself, for that is all there is of you.*
>
> – R.W. Emerson

Every entrepreneur probably needs to have some selling skills, enough to sell their idea to potential lenders or employees.

The better your self assessment, the more likely you'll surround yourself with employees and supporters whose skills complement your own.

Often a mentor is of great assistance as an advisor, objective about your skills, goals and plans. Think seriously about finding a mentor.

- **How important is money to me?**
Everyone who goes into business wants to make money. But it's crucial to decide how important money is to you. It may be difficult to sustain yourself during the long months of investing, when the notion of making money seems remote.

What are you willing to do to get financing? If you intend to remain totally independent, you probably shouldn't waste time on venture capitalists who will need to own part of your business, to share very significantly in profits, and often to participate in management.

If you can remain as a private or family business, you can probably draw more money out of it in time than if you had shareholders.

If investors, suppliers, friends and employees can identify with your values, your prospects for their financial support are improved.

- **Do you truly, passionately have the DESIRE?**
As William Bridges says in his important book *Job Shift*,[1] "Desire is the first and important ingredient of powerful motivation, and powerful motivation is essential to success."

Will I Be Able To Live With The Risk?

The decision to start a new business is not easy. There are always doubts, but because you are afraid doesn't mean you won't succeed. Good entrepreneurs recognize risks, and spend great effort minimizing them. Risk these days includes staying at a company and hoping that jobs are not eliminated.

With the uncertainty of middle management security, and the possibility of mega-mergers, downsizing and technological changes, entrepreneurship seems to be more and more attractive. This is particularly so for women who may encounter the so-called glass ceiling.

---

[1] Addison-Wesley, 1997.

Do I Really Have What It Takes?

All the questions eventually come down to: "Do I have what it takes?" Mostly this means "coping skills" because that's what you'll be called upon to do, whether it's with your banker, your suppliers, your customers, or most importantly, your family.

Do you have persistence, self-confidence, a tolerance for frugality? How do you think you'll feel signing personal guarantees, or when your paycheck seems minuscule?

Can you really live without all the support services you may be used to; the skilled word-processors, the wizards at the computer, the strong support from the sales department, etc?

Do you have what it takes? After all the questions, soul-searching, consultation, mentoring and self-analysis, there is only one way to find out.

If the need to become a woman entrepreneur burns within you, you simply have to give yourself permission to do so. You'll never forgive yourself if you don't.

I don't want to get to the end of my life
and find I've only lived the length of it.
I want to have lived the breadth of it as well.

– Unknown

What Do I Tell My Family?

This is an easy question. You tell them the truth.

You talk about your plans, what may happen to your time and availability, what may happen to the household budget. Above all, you reassure—about your love for them, and your primary commitment to their well-being.

This process is often hard for the woman entrepreneur. Your family may feel you are compromising the comforts of home. That can dilute your concentration on your business.

Unfortunately, these sorts of problems can lead to trouble for relationships. It's a tough area, but one any woman entrepreneur is wise to consider openly and at length. Identify the issues with your family and with other entrepreneurs. Explore the issues deeply. Demand honesty from yourself and others in this process.

If you do not have strong support from friends and family, you may have to reconsider your objectives. Without such support, your chances of survival and success are threatened from the beginning.

3

The Groundwork

Build Your Team

While talent, commitment and a solid product or service are a great start, the success of your business also depends on research, preparation, early financial planning and the selection of advisors. These principles apply to whatever size or type of enterprise you are planning.

Once you're ready to start your own business, you need to determine the form the business will take and the money required to get it off the ground. Assembling a team of business advisors is one excellent method of finding your way through the maze of this preparation process.

Gather Advisors

Your selection of advisors will depend on the type of business you intend to open, although almost everyone needs a lawyer and an accountant. You'll only need them part of the time, perhaps just for the start-up of your business or for major decisions.

Find good female lawyers and accountants. Seek them out because they will have a keen sense of what women entrepreneurs need, and encounter.

A lawyer should be consulted if a partnership, corporation or LLC is being formed, to advise on liability and fiduciary responsibilities, and to negotiate contracts such as leases. An accountant can help you develop record-keeping and reporting systems and in addition provide advice on financial and tax planning.

The checklist on page 188 can help you assess whether you want a particular person on your team. Remember that there's no need to select the first people you interview.

Keep looking until you find the right advisors for you, people with whom you are comfortable and who are sympathetic to your aspirations.

> *You'll go out on a limb sometimes because that is where the fruit is!*
>
> – Will Rogers

Use Outside Directors

> **Mentor Matchups**
>
> Many successful women will tell you that they wouldn't have gotten where they are without the guidance of a mentor.
>
> "Women Unlimited," a New York based organization, uses interviews and skills tests to match mentors with protégés. Call (212)572-6211.

Having a Board of Directors from outside your company is also one of the most important advisor resources you can develop, particularly if it's a family business. The concept of a Board of Directors may seem a little intimidating for a beginning entrepreneur. It needn't be. A Board of Directors can range from a very formal group, with plenty of protocol, to an informal group of trusted friends. Boards can be of any size, some so large that sub-committees are common. To begin, you might seek to establish a working group of say 4 or 5 people on whom you can call for regular meetings.

"Regular" is the key word. In the beginning, don't offer any compensation, but do spring for a good lunch, or maybe a nice working dinner over your kitchen table! The point is that you need regular advice from people interested in your progress.

You also need to be totally candid about what is going on with you and your business. Above all, be ready to accept what is said even if it does not agree with your preconceptions, and even if it bruises your ego slightly!

An outside board brings you:

- **Creativity**—You can brainstorm with your Board—Benefit from the experience and different points of view represented by Board members.
- **Objectivity**—An outside Board is a source of honest feedback. This objectivity is particularly useful for tricky items like dividends, titles, promotions, compensation and performance reviews.
- **Accountability**—Outside Boards introduce discipline and accountability to company management, often inducing better performance as a result.
- **Reassurance**—When new programs and their risks survive the scrutiny of an outside Board, company management, and employees, gain confidence in the plans.
- **Succession**—By being in place, an outside Board reassures employees, shareholders, suppliers, lenders et al, that planning for succession, particularly in a family business, will be orderly and timely.

To recruit a Board, seek respected business people in your community. They will respond because most people are flattered when you ask for their help. But think through what you want from your Board.

A quarterly meeting of 2–3 hours will be effective, and will take you a day or so to plan, but will not be too onerous a burden on the time of your Directors. Much more importantly, though, will be the promise to yourself that you are open to advice, suggestions, new ideas, even criticism. If you are not, the Board will fail.

Choose a Business Structure

You may choose to operate your business in one of several ways: as a sole proprietorship, a partnership, a corporation or (in the US) a limited liability company (LLC).

A sole proprietorship is a business owned and operated by one person. A partnership is an association of two or more people created by either a verbal or written contract. A corporation can be established by one or more people as a separate legal entity, limiting personal liability. An LLC provides the benefits of a corporation, with the tax treatment of a partnership.

Each structure has its advantages and disadvantages. Expert guidance from a lawyer and/or accountant is essential.

Criticism doesn't hurt—unless it should!

– Unknown

Start Your Financial Planning

Most businesses require a significant amount of start-up money to cover capital and operating costs including enough to pay yourself and your employees a reasonable wage, and to cover supplies and utilities until revenues start coming in.

If you are able to pay start-up costs and finance working capital needs yourself, so much the better. Most entrepreneurs need to find outside sources for financing—friends and relatives, banks, private investors or finance companies, government programs and services.

A professional approach to early financial planning will give you a head-start in convincing lenders and investors in the future. You need to be able to answer all the questions listed on page 189. If you cannot, you are not really ready to start your financial planning. You need advice, consultation and information. This is when you start to lean heavily on your advisers and outside directors, and will reap the benefit of having chosen them carefully.

Protect Your Great Ideas

Be sure your great idea remains yours. First, check if it is potentially patentable. Do a patent search at a patent library. Second, if your search shows no competing inventions, file a patent application.

To protect yourself, don't discuss your idea with anyone except trusted associates. Use a patent attorney if you prefer, but they are expensive.

It is probably easier to make a buck than to make a difference.
Both are good.

– Unknown

4

Role Model Women Entrepreneurs

Angels and a Compassionate Company

Marty took a challenge in the life of her family, "and turned it around to help other families." Marty's son Miles, born with heart, kidney and intestinal problems, has spent much of his life in hospital and has had over 30 major surgeries. When Miles was 6, he wanted "a friend who was just like him." So he and Marty created one—a rag-doll with a plastic tube from its abdomen and stitches across its heart—known as a "Shadow Buddy." On each doll, Miles wanted hearts for eyes—sending love, smiles for happiness, and his left thumbprint on the left hand of each Buddy.

Marty Postlethwait
Shadow Buddies
9875 Widman
Lenexa, Kansas
66215

From this beginning, 16 condition-specific Buddies have grown. They are 12" muslin dolls which all look the same until you peek under their hospital gowns. Many thousands of them have now been stitched, put into casts, anaesthetized, given shots, chemotherapy and loved by sick kids all over America.

Marketed to pediatric hospitals and clinics, Marty had plenty of support from family and friends, but had all the usual start-up problems including "…establishing a relationship with a banker, being a woman." But she was driven by years in hospital with Miles, and by research into pediatric illnesses. Marty "saw the need to help, to ease the pain and fears that sick children go through."

Marty now reviews her business plan "about every 3-6 months" and notes that Shadow Buddies "are doing great." Word is spreading and Marty finds that Shadow Buddy sells itself. She finds it emotional but rewarding working with sick kids, "…seeing a smile on a sick child's face is a hard won victory." Marty's business is a special project from her heart. "It helps brighten the lives of children every day… success for me is making a difference in the life of a child."

Marty's advice? "Never give up. Believe in yourself and what you do."

Role Model's Role Model

Noël Irwin-Hentschel
American Tours International Inc.
6053 West Century Blvd.
Los Angeles, California 90045

Noël Irwin-Hentschel, Chair and CEO of American Tours International, founded the company in 1977 at age 24 with life-savings of $5,000. ATI now generates $150 million in annual corporate revenues, some $2.8 billion in annual tourist revenue, while serving about one million visitors per year… "our job is to make it simpler, more efficient, and more user-friendly to visit this country," says Noël.

Noël is recognized as an outstanding business person, and has received many awards such as *Business Woman of the Year* by the National Association of Women Business Owners, the California Travel Industry Association's F. Norman Clark Entrepreneur of the Year award, and a Friend of the United Nations Humanitarian Award. She is a member of the Young Presidents Organization, and a Director of the Royal Society of Medicine Foundation.

Noël advises aspiring women entrepreneurs to learn as much as they can about their proposed business. When Noël first got into the travel business, she worked in every part of it—reservations, tours, cargo, baggage checking—the lot. "When I began our own company, I was prepared."

Drawing on experience as a mother of seven children, Noël is active with programs for learning-disabled children and the Make-A-Wish Foundation for terminally ill children.

TIME recently honored the Noël Foundation, established in 1981 to support self-sufficiency of women. Inspired by her long friendship with the late Mother Theresa, Noël says, "I've seen the entrepreneurial spirit in the poorest of women… when they are able to earn an income, and gain some self-respect, you see major changes in them."

Noël sponsors educational, entrepreneurial, health and environmental programs in America, and in countries such as: South Africa, Jordan, The Philippines, China, Pakistan, Peru, Brazil, and Somalia.

Noël's story is an inspirational example of what can be achieved by a woman entrepreneur, both in global business and international philanthropy.

Great Agonizing... Great Success

Marla Stritzel Sloan
West of the Moon
Ganges
Salt Spring Island, BC

Following her parents' example made Marla into an entrepreneur. Mother was a full-time homemaker, father a university professor. With energy to spare, and needing enough income to send their nine children to university, Marla's parents bought and renovated houses, renting them to students.

"So we kids, with parental guidance, repaired and renovated these houses—14 of them—gaining employment, and experience as a team."

Marla married, moved many miles away and had four children of her own. By the time her youngest was three, with her busy husband away a lot, Marla found herself desperate for new and challenging work. Busy at home and with no extra money, Marla agonized for seven years before committing herself to opening her own toy store. She finally summoned her resolve. "Mum, I need money—" to which the response was "How much, dear?"

Marla notes that "to have a road long denied to you, for whatever reasons, suddenly open up is a humbling experience. You realize that even though a beginning idea may spring from you, the growth and health of an endeavor rests with many people whose lives touch yours."

After hesitant first steps—"calling the landlord, asking questions, making myself visible in the community—the rest of the venture came so naturally that it was like fitting into the perfect glove. I could scarcely call it work. I had a job so interesting that I did not have to motivate myself to do it." After a short time in her first location, Marla's business grew quickly, producing a satisfactory operating profit in its first year. She was then approached by her landlord and offered her current, superb premises in a much sought after location.

Marla enjoys a strong sense of confidence in her judgment, particularly in the vital area of buying. She travels quite extensively for the business, with a discerning eye for unusual, high quality inventory.

Believing that "a good toy is a cross between great architecture and great art" Marla's philosophy about toys is deeper than just successful retailing. "Toys are a child's work, but beyond childhood, I believe that toys help support communication and intimacy in a community. That is why objects that support play at any age are important to us, and why we must always look for ways to play together. I like being involved in helping people do that."

Indomitable!

Brenda French
French Rags
11500 Tennessee Ave.
Los Angeles, CA
90064

To be a successful entrepreneur requires tenacity and courage. Brenda French has both. In 1978, with $2,000, and a creative flair, Brenda began producing knitted fashions. By 1990, she had 300 employees and annual sales of $10 million through outlets such as Saks and Bonwit. She also had slow-paying accounts and a desperate cash crunch. Her accounts receivable factor quit, cutting off cash flow. Labor problems ensued, and her company was on the brink of collapse. Brenda met one payroll from savings. She then went hiking in the Andes to think and regroup.

On her return, a New York customer offered to show Brenda's fashions to friends in her apartment. Brenda sold about $80,000 of merchandise, cash up front. Then a woman in Chicago offered to do a "trunk show," then another woman.... Brenda soon saw that work-from-home 'consultants' could reach customers who would enjoy assembling a wardrobe in a consultant's home. So now, "By appointment only" shows are conducted across America in consultant's homes; colors and styles are selected, measurements taken, deposits secured. Each garment is then custom made and shipped to the customer.

Brenda's company now has 100 consultants, 90 profit-sharing factory employees, sales of $6 million a year and climbing, lower overhead, reduced accounts receivable, everything pre-sold, no inventory but yarn, and is more profitable than ever!

One key is her business partner, Mile Rasic, whose manufacturing skill leaves Brenda to design, and to develop the home-based marketing. They have a runaway success on their hands. Plans are to grow electronically, but to keep hand-knitters for the irreplaceable detail they provide for individual customers. Brenda knows that top quality is a given for business success, and that the three magic words are now service, service, service.

Brenda comments, "...Women will not be able to change the world until they collectively have more power. Being financially independent and ultimately enjoying the power of controlling and making money brings with it the freedom to make decisions that affect others."

An Enduring Partnership

Karen Brimacombe,
Mary Halpen,
Linda Jacobsen,
Helen Miles,
Valerie Robins,
Joan Wilson
The Best of Bridge Publishing Co.
6037 6th St. SE
Calgary, AB
T2H 1L8

Over twenty years ago, these bridge-playing friends self-published the first *The Best of Bridge* cookbook. Now six titles and 2,500,000 book sales later, they are a Canadian culinary and consumer marketing phenomenon.

It began in 1975 when *The Best of Bridge* group designed a unique book format: hand-lettered recipes sprinkled with humorous sayings, full-page color pictures and a coil-bound spine, allowing the book to stay open. They convinced a national real estate company to buy their books as promotional gifts. That got them a bank loan—with no husbands' signatures. They hit the road; talked to any retailer who would listen. Decked out in recognizable aprons, they appeared on TV and radio, in supermarkets and bookstores, anywhere they could find a customer.

Unencumbered by publishing experience, these women pioneered a new approach to distribution: no returns and shipping extra. They created demand; major book chains complied. Originally the publishing neophytes packed books in boxes of 40. Not only was this too many for most book-stores, it was too heavy to lift! Convincing the store to buy a whole box was difficult. One owner quipped, "Forty books! My dear, I haven't sold that many copies of the Bible." But buy them he did, and soon ordered more. Now the books are boxed in tens, and stores are constantly asking, "When's your next book coming out?" Their latest, *That's Trump* , published in 1995, sold 160,000 copies in the first four months.

Each new book is faithful to their tradition of no-fail recipes from easy ingredients. The authors make all the decisions, and have full control over every aspect of the business. To quote the partners, "After 23 years, we're still good friends. Now, that's a success story."

1998 Update: The latest adventure, a series of six Christmas Cooking Specials for WTN (Women's Television Network) was a resounding success. More cooking shows and a new book are in the works.

Big Territories — Big Opportunities

Monique Maddy
President and CEO
African Communications Group
1 - 28 Athena Street
Cambridge
MA 02138-6036

Monique Maddy, 35, introducing state-of-the-art wireless telephone to Africa, sees this as one of the great world opportunities. From experience with the UN Development Program, Monique knew that Africa has enormous demand for telephone services. In Tanzania for example, an early 90's World Bank study reported only some 78,000 phone lines for a population of 27 million.

In 1993, her second MBA year at Harvard, Monique raised $100,000 from the UN, Motorola, Sprint, GTE and Lockheed for further African telecommunications research. She also confirmed that in meeting pent-up demand, she would face challenges from entrenched governmental monopolies.

Persevering, in November 1996 her Boston company, *African Communications Group* (ACG), installed its first 200 wireless pay phones in Dar es Salaam, Tanzania; local retailers vend company debit user cards. In January 1997 ACG won a license to compete against the government phone system in Ghana, and also started offering paging services in Tanzania.

Monique and partner Côme Laguë, a Harvard classmate, believe a new free market spirit in Africa will help lower trade barriers. Monique's vision is to provide phone service from the Mediterranean to South Africa. ACG also has requests for their services in other regions and is planning to take the concept global. One large task will be teaching consumers the benefits of telecommunication, and how to use phones.

Obtaining financing was initially difficult. After the Tanzanian pilot project proved technological and marketing feasibility, capital was more forthcoming. To expand the network into new countries, $7 million in private capital was raised. ACG also raised another $20 million, mostly in equity financing, an amount Monique expects to increase to $40 million in 1998.

Monique agrees that the African market is not yet large enough to attract global communications giants. But because of companies such as ACG, it will develop. ACG then becomes an exciting acquisition target.

Meanwhile, as Monique says: "almost wherever we go, we meet resistance... so you just have to go right in and counter it!"

Service, Service, Service... then more Service

Sunny Kobe Cook
Sleep Country USA
7029 S. 220th St.
Kent, Washington
98032

At "thirtysomething," President and CEO Sunny Kobe Cook now operates 24 Sleep Country USA stores in Seattle and Portland featuring national brand mattresses, metal beds, daybeds and adjustable beds, all at guaranteed lowest prices.

Basic homework led Sunny to develop Sleep Country USA. Loving retailing and home furnishings, Sunny's research showed that home furnishing stores earned 80% of their income from selling mattresses—but at only 20% of the investment.

Sunny's excellent merchandising includes a 60 night "Comfort Guarantee" for exchanges, and free pick-up of old mattresses upon delivery of new ones. Old mattresses are recycled to local charities; the customer is given a tax receipt. Aggressive advertising dubbed a "brilliant accident," featuring Sunny herself, combined with knowledgeable sales staff and unmatched customer service, have earned Sleep Country USA its 48% and growing Pacific Northwest market share.

Sleep Country USA so attracted a Canadian investment group that a partnership is now duplicating the concept in Canada. Of a planned 80 store Canadian chain, over 50 stores are now open in BC, Alberta and Ontario.

Sunny was Inc. Magazine's Northwest Woman Entrepreneur of the Year, a Blue Chip Enterprise winner in 1995, the Washington CEO Magazine's "Best Run Company," and Kent Chamber of Commerce Business of the Year in 1997.

Sunny works hard to develop and keep her loyal, professional, customer-oriented and smart sales people, paying above average wages and offering strong benefits. Prizes and rewards are plentiful, ranging from modest to lavish. Bonuses are paid only on a team basis, to reduce competition between employees and encourage them to build a well trained team together. Personal "thank you" and "great job" notes from Sunny reward employees who receive customer compliments.

As Sunny says during her frequent public speaking engagements, "Our business has grown so that my greatest responsibility has become rewarding and motivating those people who daily answer the phone, pay bills, sell products and make deliveries."

Dedication to Humanity

Janice Feldman (l), Carol Nicholson (r)
Rubber Rainbow Condom Co.
1182-B Robson St.
Vancouver, BC
V6E 1B2

Sisters Janice and Carol, youthful grandmothers, decided on a "Save the..." theme. But instead of forests or whales, both worthy objectives, Janice and Carol focused on humans. Janice and Carol have devoted much of their lives to joint creative projects, usually with beneficial community objectives.

In 1991, concerned about AIDS, and the health of teens, friends and families, these women went into the condom business. Distinct from any twilight zone sex shops, Carol and Janice set up colorful, tasteful shops which merchandise ONLY high quality condoms, shops which also have serious health and education objectives.

Rapidly growing Rubber Rainbow Condom Co. is their biggest effort. At this writing, stores are either open, or soon to be, in Victoria, Vancouver, Nanaimo, and Whistler in British Columbia; Edmonton, Calgary and Banff in Alberta; and Seattle, Portland, Boise and Hawaii in the US. Janice and Carol are continuously assessing applications from Canada, America and abroad.

Carol and Janice finance growth by setting up new operators in mutually approved locations for one-time lump sum fees. A contract commits the owner to selling condoms only, a store name and look, promotion and product integrity. There are no royalties or fees beyond the original set-up fee.

Control over an operator's compliance with standards comes from strong relationships between Janice and Carol and their suppliers, who, when asked, will simply cut off supplies to transgressors!

Janice and Carol are succeeding by making condoms urgent but matter-of-fact, while colorfully promoting their sale and use. Their underlying health and education missions are global.

The convictions and passions held by these two extraordinary women entrepreneurs, to "save the humans," is genuine.

As Carol and Janice said, "Well, somebody has got to do something."

Determined Excellence

Judy Resnick
Dabney, Resnick, Imperial
150 South Rodeo Dr.
Beverly Hills, CA
90212

In 1977, years after the collapse of her marriage and Judy's return to dependence on her wealthy father, he died suddenly. When she worked through his papers, she found he had cashed his life insurance, gambled away his fortune and left debts. A few months later, Judy's mother and sister died in a plane crash. At 37, Judy found she had to provide for herself and two daughters.

Judy then trusted a friend to invest proceeds from an airline settlement for her sister's and mother's death. He did that—in options, betting on the direction of stock prices. He guessed wrong. Judy lost her money.

Judy decided to become a broker herself. As a trainee she earned over $100,000 her first year and over $700,000 per year in later years. Judy invested in her brokerage. It collapsed. Judy lost her money.

In 1989, Judy borrowed from a bank and with Neil Dabney started an investment firm. As CEO, Judy was the visionary, always striving for more… faster. Staff grew from 6 to over 100. By late 1996, Judy was Chair of Dabney, Resnick, Imperial, an investment firm handling some $700 million in client assets. *The Resnick Group*, a separate company, was recently formed to give financial advice to women.

Judy describes herself as open and emotionally evolved; an "in-your-face" sort of person; she likes people and they like her. In demand as a speaker, Judy donates her time. She also holds seminars in her home, wanting to leave her mark as a teacher, a motivator, one who has shown other women some pathways to their futures.

Judy has a few rules to suggest to aspiring entrepreneurs: "seek capital, count your equity as zero, have courage… keep your integrity because it can be pretty tempting out there." Don't put total control of your money with anyone else; concentrate on financial security— "it gives personal freedom, so that you can stop being afraid."

1998 Update: In May 1997 Judy sold her interest in the brokerage, focusing on her investment management firm, *The Resnick Group.* Judy has also completed a book titled, *I've Been Rich. I've Been Poor. Rich is Better*, Golden Books, 1988. [I've read it—Good book! – Author]

Spectacular Location... Creative Results

Danna Britton
Boardwalk Greens
Ganges
Salt Spring Island, BC
V8K 2L3

Danna's 12' x 14' *Boardwalk Greens* garden and patio gift store has a world-class location overlooking Ganges Harbour on Salt Spring Island, a port of choice for pacific Northwest boating enthusiasts. Festooned with wonderful hanging baskets grown by the owner, and offering classy garden/patio furniture, statuary and decor items, this is a thriving seasonal business, often photographed and featured in print media.

Originally planning to return to school for an accounting degree, single mother Danna found the cost of doing so too formidable. Working with the Salt Spring Island Parks and Recreation Department, then venturing into her own gardening and maintenance business, Danna's garden shop "just happened." She found her magical location and hasn't looked back.

Danna spotted a niche. Salt Spring Islanders, attuned to nature and gardens, are sometimes over-ambitious in creating gardens. The gardens become successful and soon, too big to be cared for comfortably! Danna's specialty became "container gardening," providing planters and plants that pare down gardening work to something more manageable.

Danna supplements seasonal garden store income by doing store displays, interior decorating and painting rubber boots! Using special (secret!) paint, Danna turns rubber boots into colorful, unique fashion accessories, often as custom designs. She has shipped boots all over the world.

Danna, a survivor, left home at 15 and did whatever menial but decent jobs she could find to support herself. She describes herself as determined, resourceful and creative. Danna is certainly all of those.

1998 Update: After 5 years, Danna has hired a part-time garden store manager and another boot decorating artist. Danna now also successfully represents one of her suppliers of garden pots, quickly becoming the Company's leading salesperson in Canada. She is considering new *Boardwalk Greens* locations and suggests: "work hard, keep smiling and be determined."

5

Develop Opportunities

Previous chapters touched upon the skills you need to develop your business. But what if you have no ideas to which you can apply these skills? If you've come this far, you'll certainly now find ideas to consider. It's a process of looking around, asking questions, and opening your mind to possibilities. Brainstorming business ideas is an excellent technique, where one idea will lead to another.

Generate Ideas and Identify Opportunities

Many people think that all you need to start a business is one good idea. However, ongoing business success often depends upon the ability to produce ideas and innovation on a continuing basis. This ensures that a business stays in touch with the marketplace. Business owners who watch for possible new products, services, procedures and processes keep their businesses healthy. Without growth and new ideas, any business will die.

Identifying business opportunities combines analysis with creativity. Some business owners are skilled at carrying out this process on their own, while others may want to assemble a "team"—people with different talents and skills who can interact to produce ideas and evaluate their potential. Many books on creative thinking and brainstorming are available in libraries and book stores.

Some ideas that are working these days include retail security stores, selling everything relevant to home safety and security; brew-your-own beer and wine shops; candy stores which recognize that the sweet tooth is back. Concerns about aging have spawned many "rejuvenation" products and services, such as home gym equipment and exercise videos.

A long list of other ideas to start you thinking appears on page 190.

You see things and say, "Why?"
I dream of things that never were and say, "Why not?"

– G.B. Shaw

Testing Business Ideas

Basic Considerations

An idea is a business opportunity only if it has a chance for success. You may think of 100 ideas, but only one or two may have sufficient merit to be an opportunity. To determine whether a business idea is an opportunity, four basic questions must be answered:

- **Personal…** Will the proposed activities satisfy your personal and financial goals?
- **Marketing…** Can you show that the products or services have real potential for success?
- **Production…** Can you produce the products or services, marketable at competitive prices?
- **Financial…** Can you obtain the capital and operating financing needed?

Collect Information

To assure yourself that a business idea can meet your goals, you will need considerable information. Good sources include:

- local chambers of commerce
- existing businesses
- purchasing agents, suppliers, wholesalers
- company annual reports
- trade association literature
- government publications
- market research reports
- Yellow Pages
- libraries
- industry contacts
- specialized trade books

Additional information may be obtained by:

- conducting telephone and personal surveys
- observing competitive business activities and facilities
- becoming a customer of potential competitors
- producing sample products; test market trials

Ask Questions

The questions on page 191 will help you to determine whether a particular idea merits further consideration. Testing new venture ideas is a skill developed with practice. At first, you may find the questions difficult, but after you have used them a few times, your skills will increase.

If after answering these questions, you are confident that your idea has a good chance of succeeding, develop a full business plan and continue your market research. If possible, start with the actual selling of the product or service on a small scale. This is excellent market research.

Test Ideas While Moonlighting

You've heard the old saying: "Don't quit your day job!"

With downsizing and restructuring convulsing big business, a safety net is a good idea. Smart employees realize they may need a whole portfolio of skills to survive, not just one. Developing a side business is one good way to develop this portfolio.

Developing a side business requires discipline and organization. But the reward is great—You prepare yourself emotionally, practically and financially for the leap into entrepreneurship. You'll land on your feet with many new needs all lined up—money, equipment and customers.

Choosing the business can be difficult however. It must merge with your current job, i.e. not require daytime hours, 24-hour attention or much travel.

Before you pursue this whole idea, determine your company's policy towards moonlighting. If your company forbids it, then you are better advised to do just preparatory steps: everything except actually earning money. Then when you do step out, you can concentrate almost entirely on earning money.

A major advantage of moonlighting is that you can test ideas. You can discuss and cure weaknesses in an idea, or abandon it without putting you or your company at too much risk. You can keep trying ideas until one works.

> *Be a part of the change you want to see in the world.*
>
> – Unknown

Ethical Strategy

In the meanwhile, the proper, ethical strategy in your day job is to be the exemplary employee, doing excellent work, being highly visible and even volunteering for extra tasks. Recognize that you do have an obligation to the company that's currently paying your way, and letting you plan your way into entrepreneurship. When you leave, you want it to be honorably. After all, your former employer could become your biggest customer.

> *We have to stop making things that sell and make things that help.*
>
> – Mary Pipher, "In the Shelter of Each Other," Ballantine, 1997, p. 266.

6

Explore Creative Opportunities

What's New

North Americans are the ultimate consumers. But things are changing. Buyers can no longer always afford to purchase "new" simply on impulses. Real value and genuine service are what consumers seek today.

Consider the rapid growth of "new to you" resale shops. These stores appeal to buyers seeking bargains, and to entrepreneurs who appreciate the low original capital outlay. But according to veterans of the business, anything less than a six month initial survival fund is dangerous, because these businesses tend to have slow starts.

Longevity, and the quality of it, are huge concerns of baby boomers, those consumers born between 1946 and 1964. Thus, products and services involved with health issues, such as nutrition and fitness, represent huge opportunities for entrepreneurs.

Witness the explosion in exercise machines, TV fitness programs and fitness facilities. Note also pesticide-free and organically grown foods, packaged with new standards of sanitation and environmental responsibility.

Technology of shopping is also rapidly evolving. TV is changing the way many consumers shop. This translates into new distribution opportunities for entrepreneurs, including those now operating in traditional ways and those seeking new ways to appeal to consumers.

Entrepreneurs are also capitalizing on changes in corporate habits. Temporary employment agencies are booming as business takes advantage of the economies and flexibility of "temp" help.

"Outsourcing" is a key concept in business today, causing concern and attrition in unions. Outsourcing results in the creation of myriad small companies offering specialized services ranging from computer servicing to cleaning and maintenance.

Trends—See page 194 for succinct descriptions of 16 North American consumer social trends identified in Faith Popcorn's 1996 book *Clicking*.[1] Read the book for elaboration on these trends. Consider the entrepreneurial possibilities and opportunities in each of these trends.

---

[1] Harper Collins, 1996.

How About Buying an Existing Business?

There are a number of good reasons for purchasing an existing business. There are also a number of real dangers for the unwary.

Among the advantages:

- The purchasing of an existing customer and supplier base, a proven location, trained employees, tested products and services. Contracts, permits, licenses are in place, trade credit relationships are established. Often, the existing owner will stay on for a while as an invaluable mentor.
- Financing is often more flexible. The vendor may be willing to help with some or all of the financing. If the vendor retains a minority stake in the business, perhaps the initial cash required can be less, in return for a vendor's option to sell the minority position to you or others after a defined period of time.
- Financing may be easier because of existing assets available for collateral. Lenders often regard existing businesses as more controllable risks than start-up ventures.

The difficulty is finding the healthy business that suits you. Lawyers, accountants, insurance agents and bankers are usually among the first to know if a business is for sale, and are professionals you should canvass.

Business brokers, while knowledgeable, are usually bound to represent the interests of the vendor who is paying their fee, and therefore may not be totally objective.

Your lawyer and accountant should review financial statements, income tax records for the last several years, leases, contracts, etc., early in the process to detect problems which may reveal why the business is for sale and whether any of the information is incomplete or misleading.

Independent appraisals can be a worthwhile investment to determine the health of equipment, accuracy of inventory counts and valuations, age of accounts receivable, etc.

Key employees should be interviewed. Will they be staying on? Do you **want** them staying on, and if not, what difficulties do you face for terminations?. Suppliers and customers are good sources of information about the general state of the business.

There is an enormous range of questions to be answered when looking at a business that attracts you. Sometimes a purchaser can be a little starry-eyed, particularly if there is the suggestion that another buyer is waiting in the wings. Here, once again, is the need for cold, unhurried objectivity from advisors, mentors and professionals.

Import An Idea

North America does not have the corner on new or different products and services. When traveling in your own or other countries, be alert for successful local ideas that appeal to you.

When you do spot something you feel you might like to consider, study how you might do it. Perhaps you just arrange to import an item. There is plenty of free advice available as to permits and procedures.

Or investigate an agreement to become a licensed manufacturer; or design an improvement. Study a service, see what market niche it serves—or a niche for which you can adapt it.

Second-hand Ideas!

The dead ideas of others are a common source of new business ventures. Reborn ideas have many advantages. Cost is one. Inventories of failed products can often be bought at a fraction of their original cost, as can the tools and dies to make them.

An astute entrepreneur can learn from project history, then change things for another approach. An often crucial advantage is to have artwork, printed materials, and other marketing tools thrown in.

Often, the economies of scale necessary for a product's success cannot be achieved in the big company which has spent all the up-front development money, thereby providing an opportunity for a niche marketer.

One of the biggest reasons for failed products is lack of imagination and innovation from the original marketer. For instance, a product which failed at regular retail could be a winner by mail-order.

Look around at work for failed products, watch for bankruptcy notices, scan trade journals for information on products which failed, research patent records—Millions of patents are on library data bases.

Most patented products never reach the market. You could also come across an old patent for something good today, and on which the 17-year patent protection has elapsed.

Of course, as in any entrepreneurial activity, there are risks to this approach for finding "new" products. Is there a stigma, unresolved credit or legal problems attached to the previous failure? Have you got the resources, or can you get them, for a previously unsuccessful idea? Can you learn enough to make it work in today's market?

Obviously, caution and research are still key words.

Should You Buy A Franchise?

Blue chip franchises look attractive and certainly have a high rate of success. They often require big dollars though—$250,000 and more is not uncommon for well-known ones. That doesn't include working capital for everyday operating needs.

There are a number of basic issues to consider:

- **Do you want to be boss or a manager?**
  Big franchises became that way by insisting that you adhere to detailed, precise, day-to-day operating standards. Thus in essence, you become a manager. If the prospect of that much control over your business doesn't appeal, you need to look very carefully at big-name franchises.
- **Will you wait?**
  For the top franchises, there are often waiting lists. When openings do develop, they may be some distance away. Are you willing to move to buy a franchise?

Some franchisors want you to work for them for a while before they'll sell you a franchise. In that case, you could end up not qualifying. That would be frustrating but may be a good thing, both for you and the franchisor.

Smaller, newer franchises are not so expensive and they may have more flexibility. But in these cases, you may become part of overall growth experience of newer operations, experience gained through your pain.

If you do decide to look at a franchise, pay for expert advice from your lawyer and accountant. They can help you avoid bad deals.

Many individuals getting into franchising are surplus staff from corporate down-sizing. To them, franchising can represent some of the independence they now crave—but with some of the support systems that they are used to relying on in the corporate world, such as in financing and marketing.

One category of franchising logical for all corporate refugees, but particularly friendly for women, is business-to-business services. Businesses serving other businesses are a growth leader among franchisors.

This business-to-business category obviously coincides with the rapid expansion of the small business market. Service-to-business franchises include accounting, advertising, promotion, publicity, employee training and personnel services.

If you are inclined to look at a franchise in the business services field, remember—all cautions still apply—examine franchisor financial health, franchisee turnover, start-up costs and royalties. Will you be boss or manager? Obtain advice.

Questions to ask about franchises are listed on page 196.

Great New Long-Term Entrepreneurial Opportunities

Global warming will worsen earth's problems—perhaps not in your lifetime, but certainly in that of today's children—as explained in *The Heat Is On*, by Ross Gelbspan[1]. Gelbspan suggests the world must switch from carbon-dioxide producing fossil fuels—gas, oil, coal—to non-polluting renewable fuels, such as hydrogen and solar energy. The technology exists.

This changeover process will create investment and employment world-wide, compromise between 'have/have-not' nations, and huge entrepreneurial opportunities. Visualize converting to clean fuels every vehicle, plane, train, ship, home, building and factory on earth.

On a gentler note, visualize school children planting trees in their communities, helping to replace carbon-monoxide consuming trees gone from world forests. [Could you, with other parents, organize that now in **your** children's schools? I believe you could attract volunteer families to help, and raise funds from business and government.]

Please read about Global Warming.

World Population

Another of humanity's problems is said to be the rapidly expanding population, particularly in third world countries. Good news on this topic comes from UN research.[2] Since the 1950's, the average world fertility rate has declined. Fertility rates have dropped below replacement rates in many developing countries, including Cuba, China, Thailand, and probably soon, in Brazil.

There is a direct correlation between the education of young women and the reduction of the birth rate. UNICEF states that for every extra year a girl stays in school, fertility and child mortality rates drop and wages increase.

Population stabilization is a key to many global problems. There simply must be entrepreneurial opportunities for women to help other women world-wide to obtain education, better nutrition, sanitation, clean water, and raised living standards. For instance, assisting women to establish their own businesses will help them become self-sufficient, provide better education for their children. Microloan programs and mentoring for these women entrepreneurs could be invaluable.

---

1 Addison-Wesley, 1997.

2 Reported on page A15 of the 4/11/98 issue of the Victoria, BC., Times Colonist newspaper, by College Educator Karen Hodgson.

Some Don'ts

If you look through the classifieds of almost any business or success publication, you will find ads offering you the chance to make enormous amounts of money, usually without much work and certainly in hardly any time at all.

It's fun to answer a few of these ads. The material you receive is often very well written, so compelling that you will likely succumb to one or two pitches, regardless of what is said here. That's okay, we've all done it. Just don't buy into too many!

As soon as possible, though, decide to recognize and accept the truth when it is offered to you. The truth is that for an entrepreneur to make money **you must originate your own product or service!**

Among the "business opportunities" to avoid, you will see countless:

- **Blind ads —** Those which offer overnight riches, but won't tell you what they're selling. They'll share their secrets with you for a fee. Nonsense!
- **Catalogs** — Pre-printed catalogs of novelties or books. You buy the catalogs, send them out to people on purchased mailing lists (incredible booby traps of their own), and wait for orders. Keep 50%, send 50% to the catalog suppliers; they then ship the merchandise to your customer. Sounds foolproof but it doesn't work. Your 50% margin is not enough to cover costs of advertising and mailing lists.
- **Import/Export** — A hugely complex business; very large, well-entrenched companies are in this business. Unless you have time and money to visit countries all over the world to do the purchasing, you can't compete.
- **Multi-Level** — Many multi-level marketing concepts are good but study the statistics. The "people failure" rate is enormous.
- **Work-at-Home** — Usually lots of hype, fees for big promises and no substance, no real guidance, and often just scams.
- **Some Others** — Cash in on government programs; borrow huge sums overnight; fix your credit; envelope stuffing; home assembly; read books or watch TV for money, etc. The list is endless.

To repeat, for an entrepreneur to make money **you need to originate your own product or service!** You have to be the source. That's it. That's truth.

> *A life spent in making mistakes is not only more honorable, but much more useful than a life full of doing nothing.*
>
> – G.B. Shaw

7

Should You Operate From Home?

Is Working At Home for You?

> A university study revealed that roughly three quarters of home-based businesses have not conducted a formal feasibility study, developed projected financial statements, or done a separate marketing plan.
> Please don't be one of them!

Home-based business is one of the fastest growing forms of entrepreneurship. With computer and communications technology, the home is now a practical workplace.

The NFWBO estimates that, as of 1994, 3.5 million women-owned firms are home-based. Nearly two-thirds (63%) of these firms provide full or part-time employment for 14 million people in addition to the owner.

Running a successful home-based business requires a viable idea, common sense, dedication, sound advice and proper business planning.

Is one type of person more suited to working at home than another? Definitely. Temperament is a critical factor for being happy and productive at home.

A person who can answer "yes" to most of the questions on page 197 is more likely to prosper working from home than one who cannot.

Assessing the Home Front

Personal and family considerations are important to the success of most businesses. They become even more critical in a home-based situation. Consider the following as possible influences on you and your business success:

Reasons for Starting a Home-Based Business

Why do you want to start or run a home-based business in the first place? Motivating factors include:

- being your own boss, avoiding regimentation
- spending more time with, or being in the same place as your family
- having time for other interests
- wanting to expand a hobby or an interest.

- avoiding commuting problems and expense
- making money

Personal Qualities and Traits

Business is one area in which success is determined by faith in yourself, self-confidence and self-esteem, qualities which can be strengthened and developed.

Most people gain confidence as they do something successfully a number of times. Consider investing some time to build your confidence and self-esteem, as part of your preparation for business.

> **Avoid Isolation!**
>
> 1. Join the Chamber of Commerce.
> 2. Plan business meetings outside your home.
> 3. Arrange your schedule so that you keep up social contacts.
> 4. Spend good quality time with the family.
> 5. Plan get-togethers with former co-workers.
> 6. Attend business-related seminars, workshops or trade shows.

Some possible ways are training yourself to concentrate on your positives and your successes, taking community education courses to build confidence, joining a group such as a speakers, professional or business club, and investing in self-improvement seminars.

See the self-help section in your local library.

Personal Resources

Create an inventory of resources available to you: energy, enthusiasm, time, training, sales experience, personal contacts, support and possible financing from friends, savings, investments, your partner's income, income from the job you may keep during start-up. Then make plans to use all the resources.

Successful business people usually draw on other people as resources. Learning to see people as resources may require a shift in your perspective.

Home Base and Home Life

> **Parental Survival**
>
> List all the fun things you've cut back on since you had kids and/or started your business. Then plan on doing one of them at least once a week.

Some home-based businesses fail because family members have different ideas about what is important and about the effects the business will have on the family. Talk about these matters openly with family members involved. Do research to identify the issues, and possible solutions, as the basis for these vital family discussions.

A home-based business can absorb all your time and energy. There is a risk that as you devote so much time to your business, other parts of your life will be ignored.

You may become a workaholic! If managed, that energy can help make a business succeed. Ignored, workaholism, like other addictions, isolates people from family and friends and causes stress. In serious cases, this can lead to family breakdown and business failure.

Many women struggle to strike a balance between business and household work. Expectations in this area, seldom discussed and often perceived differently by household members, must be brought out in the open.

When a woman is known to be at home, even though heavily engaged in running a business, others may find it reasonable to ask that a little extra be done here or there by her. These patterns can undermine business success.

Check out expectations and possible effects on your business and household with your family/partner. Discuss them often and openly.

Don't let problems fester. See the *Sharing Quotient Quiz*, page 197.

Essential Space

The need for a designated space for the home business, even if severely restricted, is vital. Sometimes more symbolic than real, it does make a statement about the seriousness of your undertaking.

Assess the physical layout of your home—Where might you be able to conduct business? What remodeling might have to be done?

Estimates will be necessary in your business plan for location, premises, facilities and start-up costs.

Is Home the Best Place?

Is home best for the business you have in mind? Some potential advantages and disadvantages of a home base include:

Potential Advantages

- opportunity to use household resources for business
- low overhead, running costs
- gradual start-up and growth
- no commuting time or expense
- tax advantages
- lower risk of mistakes
- relatively inexpensive way to test a market
- reduced child-care costs; increased quality time with family

Potential Disadvantages

- isolation and lack of contact with business colleagues
- increased family stress; difficulty separating business and home life
- need for self-discipline to plan and manage one's own time
- by-laws and regulations affecting what you can and can't do from home
- poor image (you may look more home-like than business-like)
- conflict with neighbors over noise, traffic, and changed use of space

Finding Home-Based Business Opportunities

Make a list of ideas that seem to be good opportunities. Edit to a core list. Get opinions from family and friends. Choose one idea to assess, and if research shows it isn't a real opportunity, examine another.

An "idea" becomes an "opportunity" when it has a chance to succeed as a business. Enabling you to assess a business idea's chances of success is the purpose of research—and most of this book. See page 198 for some home-based business ideas.

Turn Your Interests Into Home Based Opportunities

Prospective home based entrepreneurs often make the mistake of narrowing their choices too quickly, starting the first business that comes to mind. Try to come up with several ideas for businesses. The object is to discover business opportunities that will not only be profitable, but personally rewarding, too.

Interests Can Become Income

1. Jot down interests, hobbies, leisure activities, plus work or volunteer experience you've enjoyed. (For example, traveling, collecting miniatures, cooking, chopping, fishing, working with computers, meeting people).
2. Try to convert an interest into an income. For example, if you like to ski and travel, you might organize ski charters; or if you're interested in photography and enjoy meeting people, perhaps a videotaping service would work.
3. Narrow the list down to three or four businesses that appeal to you the most.
4. Research these further. Who would your customers be? How do you reach them? Who is your competition? How much money will you need to get started? Use this book as a guide to help you with these research questions.

Complete the four steps noted above and you may be surprised. A business that seemed like a good idea might not remain on your list. Conversely, an activity you've always done purely for fun could emerge as a potential money-maker.

Match the business to your preferences, not vice-versa. Do what you love to do—The money will follow!

Things You Need to Know Before You Start

Insurance

You cannot rely on your homeowner's insurance if you have a home-based business. Working at home can change your insurance risk in a big way. Talk to your insurance agent about taking care of this.

Home-based business experts stress early research into zoning, bylaws and regulations. Enquire at any chamber of commerce, business information center or government agent's office in your community. You don't want to get all fired up about an idea only to discover zoning or by-law problems that restrict you. Regulations that affect home-based businesses exist at all levels of government: federal, regional and local.

Federal and Regional Governments

Federal and regional regulations cover general matters, such as fair business practices, reporting to them, and consumer protection on advertising, packaging and labeling. Both the federal and regional levels of government levy personal and business taxes.

Local Government

Local by-laws cover zoning; where different types of businesses may operate, and local operating requirements. Zoning spells out what is and isn't allowed as a business from a home in your area. This really does mean you!

> **Home Office Tax Advice**
>
> You can deduct the expenses of running the space you use in your home exclusively for your business. But home-based business expenses are among the riskiest tax deductions you can claim. They are scrutinized by the income tax folks because of the frequency of abuse. The key words are use of space "regularly" and "exclusively" for business.
>
> You are best advised to obtain tax advice, and to follow rules to the letter! The amount you may save by chiseling a little will never be worth the aggravation and the never-ending scrutiny you might attract.

Licenses and Permits

Conducting a business usually requires licenses and permits. Trade and professional associations, licensing boards and local planning or economic development offices are sources of licensing and permit information.

Assessing Possible Changes

Consider the influences of a home-based business by writing an explanation of how the business will affect your life—family, social, professional, personal. Include ideas for dealing with negative effects. Discuss what you have written with family, friends and advisors.

The success of the home-based enterprise largely depends on the support of family. Keep them informed early and reduce the stresses of start-up.

To assess whether starting a home-based business is realistic for you, work through the range of questions beginning on page 201.

8

The Dream Comes Alive

Once you've assembled advisors, and mapped out financial requirements, it's time to choose your business structure, to complete legal, licensing and registration requirements and to prepare to obtain financing. Be aware that your financial institution normally will not lend you 100% of your start-up financing. Your lender will require that you invest some of your own money as a symbol of your commitment. If you need outside financing, that means preparing an organized, professional presentation—detailed information about yourself and your business.

It is normal for the lender to request supporting security or collateral, such as a personal guarantee, a statement of personal net worth for yourself (and perhaps your spouse), and in some instances, a mortgage or outside security to support guarantees.

All financial institutions require a business plan—a document that states how you plan to achieve your goals. Financial institutions will also require considerable personal information about you in order to judge your talents, skills and chance of success.

Once you have a business plan and details of your personal information, you are ready to meet with your financial institution. The business plan helps establish credibility for the business. But be prepared; the institution will be mainly interested in repayment, and assets as security to help guarantee that.

Preparing to Prepare Your Business Plan

A business plan is an outline of facts about your business—its structure, goals, marketing, operational and financial requirements. It shows that you have thoroughly researched and planned your new business.

On page 203 is a checklist to help you confirm that you have enough information to begin preparing your business plan. You need answers to many, many questions. If you do not have answers to the questions, you need to do more research and to consult your advisors. Set out in Appendices I and II (page 165), are references to sources of information to assist you in finding answers to your business plan questions.

A business plan will describe in detail your product or service, your target customers, marketing plans and proposed suppliers. It will show estimated revenue, expenses, profit potential, start-up capital needed, and working capital resources required. You will need enough money to cover "start-up" costs and at least six months' operating expenses. Entrepreneurs also usually save enough money to cover personal expenses for six months or more. Your business plan should show time requirements.

Whether you are seeking to get your new business running, or whether you are looking to expand your existing business, you probably need to raise capital. Where do entrepreneurs turn?

What Investors Seek in a Business Plan

To convince an investor to finance your dream, you need a feet-on-the-ground business plan. Here's what all investors look for in a business plan, be they flinty bankers or warm friends:

- **A mission statement** — a few simple clear well-turned sentences which explain who you are and what you are going to do.
- **An executive summary** — about a page, summarizing the most important points in your plan. These include your mission statement; descriptions of your company, management, short and long-term goals; a statement of how much money you seek and your plan for repaying it. Your objective for this executive summary page is to get your reader to read page 2 and beyond.
- **A concise document** — about 50 pages maximum, void of jargon, unnecessary charts and puffery.
- **Realistic financial projections** — base numbers on fact, not fantasy. Really work on your qualitative assumptions. Err on the conservative side with operating costs, sales forecasts, gross profit margins, management compensation, working capital requirements, etc.
- **The management team** — this key area gets close scrutiny. Any misrepresentation, however innocent, risks the integrity of the whole proposal. If prior management experience—a key ingredient—is thin, bolster your management with a board of directors which includes an expert, perhaps retired, in your business.

Questions Every Lender Asks

- **How much do you need?** Don't be coy. Be specific about the amount you are seeking. Set the framework for your negotiations; show how well you understand your business.
- **What do you want it for?** Working capital? A marketing blitz? Start-up funding? Different sources favor different objectives and have differing tolerances for risk.

- **How will the money improve your business?** Lenders want to see you move towards being self-sustaining and will need to know how their money moves you towards that. You need credible projections showing: lowered costs, or improved volume, or improved working capital, or expanded capacity, etc. resulting from use of their money.
- **When will you pay the loan back?** Use your cash flow projections to show when the loan should pay off for you—and therefore when and how you can start paying it back. Be specific.
- **What is your back-up plan?** If the business runs into trouble, secured lenders try to liquidate their collateral. But if you can reassure equity lenders, who don't have that alternative, that you have other options for revenue, or cutting costs, or financing, this will greatly improve your original chances for financing approval.

Meeting With Potential Lenders

Have informal meetings with potential lenders to discuss different loan arrangements and other aspects of financing required for your business. At these meetings, your lenders will want to learn about you, giving you a chance to show your commitment and expertise. Once your business plan is ready and you've decided what financing is right for you, arrange formal meetings with the most promising lenders.

The checklist on page 204 will help you prepare for these meetings by listing common questions asked by lenders. Consult with your team of advisors if your answers aren't almost all "yes" Recognize that lenders compete with each other so don't be afraid to shop!

Commercial Banks

Commercial banks give lip-service to funding start-up businesses and will often go over your business plan, making useful comments. However, few make actual business loans to young companies unless heavily secured by third party signatures and other assets.

This situation probably won't change. A banker judges very simply: Will they get the bank's money back? New borrowers, with short or non-existent track records, often have a hard time convincing loans officers that the money will be repaid as planned.

In addition, the woman entrepreneur may perceive a chauvinist reticence on the part of lenders simply because she is a woman. Stories abound of the need for a husband's signature, etc.

On the other hand, some studies have shown that chauvinism is sometimes seized upon by women as an excuse for failure to obtain financing, when the real truth is that a good sound proposal, thoroughly prepared and documented, was not presented.

So concentrate on the advice of your advisors, the excellence of your research and proposal presentation. Look to these if you are hoping to finance your venture through a loan. Use the emotional energy generated from a turndown for the extra research, knowledge and planning that will strengthen your next presentation.

Remember that experienced loans officers listen to the dreams of entrepreneurs as part of their routine. They simply do not share your emotional high for your project. Sure, loans officers will look for passion and commitment, but those alone will not make your case.

As guardians of someone else's money, loans officers must be hard-nosed about your estimates, forecasts, sources of information, crisis planning, etc. Rose-colored glasses just never have fit on loans officers. (And since you probably keep your own funds in a bank somewhere, you want to be very glad they don't.)

Private Investors

More and more, private investors are seen as the best source of financing for start-up ventures. These can be anyone anywhere—relatives, friends or strangers. Commonly, these are people who want to earn more on their money than is available on "safe" but low-yield investments.

Generally, private investors are just that—individuals operating on their own, knowing what they like and dislike, and listening for opportunities through personal and other contacts.

Thus, the challenge for the entrepreneur seeking investor financing is to be able to find investors and then make sound proposals to the right individuals. This takes organized effort, and involves canvassing virtually everyone you know. You never know where and when a lead will appear.

But there will always be two basic criteria. Investors must be satisfied about the industry in which you want them to invest, and they must be satisfied about your management skills.

It makes sense therefore to concentrate on:

- people who have confidence in you
- people who know something about the business you propose
- people who might enjoy some personal involvement in your business.

Private investors generally look for equity (ownership) in any business they fund, as part compensation for loaning start-up or working capital funds.

This gives investors a way of being able to share in the profits you expect to. They will be looking for pretty hefty returns (profit sharing) on their equity money. But in turn, well-connected investors can often open doors for you.

Finance Companies

Many start-up companies turn to finance companies. These lenders are less regulated than banks and don't answer to inspectors. Finance companies can make credit decisions based on the quality of a company's assets, e.g. accounts receivable, or finished goods in inventory. This increases the chances of a loan. Be aware though that a finance company's interest rates can be high, usually several percentage points over the bank prime rate. But, they are there if you can afford them. (Legendary real estate developer, Bill Zeckendorf, once observed that it is sometimes better to be alive at 6% over prime, or more, rather than dead at prime!)

Other Possible Sources

- **Angels.** While angels are known for being interested in equity, there's no standard formula. Advice from your lawyer and accountant is essential.
- **Private Placements.** Some investment firms find investors you may not find on your own. Ask your accountant or lawyer for an introduction.
- **Customers and Suppliers.** While many people turn to customers and suppliers as a last resort, some seek out those sources early. If you can come up with an incentive to get your customers to pay sooner or get your suppliers to cut you more slack on your accounts payable, you can get by with less outside financing.
- **Leasing.** Leasing can be a means of acquiring equipment without borrowing money. Equipment makers with financing capabilities usually offer good terms to stimulate sales.

In The US

- **State Programs.** More than half the States have revolving loan funds for working capital and fixed-asset requirements at attractive terms. A number have loan-guarantee programs. Typically, they're coordinated by local economic-development officials in State government offices.
- **US Small Business Administration.** Probably the first place a woman entrepreneur in the US should turn to get information on how to finance her new business is to the US Small Business Administration (SBA). The SBA will guide and direct the entrepreneur towards funding sources.

  Many entrepreneurs have received help from the SBA. The SBA does not provide funds directly, but rather co-signs loans provided by commercial lenders. The SBA seeks borrowers of good character, commitment, management experience and ability to repay. An SBA-guaranteed loan has a good chance of being approved, because it is judged more on credit history and character than on assets or collateral.

  Several major SBA initiatives are designed for women. Women applicants should seek information on:
  - The Women's Prequalification Pilot Loan Program. This allows the SBA to pre-approve a loan up to $250,000 to the woman business owner, before she goes to the bank!
  - Training, management assistance and mentoring programs specifically for women entrepreneurs. There are Small Business Development Centers nationwide, with over 1,000 service locations.
  - Other SBA financial assistance programs. These are of relevance to women entrepreneurs:
    - The 7(a) Loan Guarantee
    - The Low-Documentation 7(a) Loan
    - Fastrak Pilot Project
    - Caplines
    - International Trade and Export Working Capital Loans
    - The 504 Certified Development Company Loans
    - The Small Business Investment Company Network.

  Clearly, SBA assistance deserves considerable study beyond the scope of these remarks and references. Obtain guidance on all programs from the SBA "Answer Desk."

  The SBA accepts applications by fax as well as by mail. Call the SBA Answer Desk in Washington, DC.

In Canada

As in many countries, there are serious resources available in Canada for aspiring entrepreneurs, many particularly for women entrepreneurs.

A typical federal program is one sponsored by Human Resources Development Canada (HRDC). Working through local offices across Canada, for third party delivery through many provincial agencies, HRDC actively promotes a "Self-Employment Benefit" encouraging the development and presentation of plans for new entrepreneurial businesses by applicants who are on income assistance. Successful applicants can qualify for income support.

An example of this type of agency is the "Victoria Women Work Society." This non-profit society in Victoria, British Columbia, funded by HRDC, provides entrepreneurial training programs for single mothers. A "micro-loan" program is available to help graduates get underway, as is follow-up business counseling and mentorships with local business women.

Private industry is also involved. An initiative to sponsor young entrepreneurs was recently launched by two of Canada's big banks, the Royal Bank and the Canadian Imperial Bank of Canada. The Canadian Youth Business Foundation (CYBF) is designed to assist young people lacking financing and experience, to put their ideas to work.

In the field of education, the Etobicoke Board of Education, (in a suburb of Toronto, Ontario) is opening a business entrepreneurial academy in September 1998. The "Scarlett Heights Collegiate Institute" will start infusing into the Grade 9 curriculum training in such skills as planning, decision-making, team building, networking, goal setting, and risk taking. Additional curricula will be added into each grade, each year, through to high school graduation. These skills, attitudes and attributes will be taught by dedicated and knowledgeable teachers, with strong support from business and the community.

Among the most meaningful programs are those involving women volunteer mentoring groups. There are innumerable variations of this strategy, certainly across North America, and probably world-wide. One such group is described in the following:

Wired Woman Society[1]

Entrepreneur — Woman — Volunteer — The Connections are Clear

The number of professional women who volunteer is high. Women want to give back to their community, to make it a better place to live. This is a phenomenon which is to be encouraged.

As mentioned earlier in this book, a study by the National Foundation for Women Business Owners (NFWBO) showed that 78% of women business owners participate in volunteer activities—a significantly higher rate than the average adult.

One such volunteer organization in Vancouver, British Columbia, is the "Wired Woman Society." There are over 300 members, the majority of whom are self-employed professionals, ranging from accountants and bankers to system analysts and multi-media specialists—a great cross-section of skilled working women and women entrepreneurs. These women provide high-quality opportunities for women and girls to learn about new media and digital technologies.

So why do members of the Wired Woman Society, who could just take their money and time and do other things, donate their time and money to improving the skills of women?

A 1992 focus Group Report from the University of California's Women and Philanthropy Program suggests that women have personal, subjective reasons such as:[2]

- the need to give, and the personal impact from doing so.
- the need to give money and time.
- for personal involvement in organizations and activities.
- to make a difference.

Women also volunteer for good sound business reasons—such as networking for their business, control over self and professional development, and flexible time management.

Non profit organizations such as the Wired Woman Society depend on tangible contributions from government, the public and corporations. But the work and the power required to implement such outreach projects comes from people giving their time for free. The majority of people willing to do this are women.

---

[1] The *Wired Woman Society*, by member Carolyn Prentice.

[2] Source: homepages.together.net/-akakii/womenphl.htm

Women entrepreneurs volunteering has progressed naturally from the traditional situation where housewives were the predominant volunteering demographic. The advantages of being self-employed have extended the ability of women to give their time to grassroots causes.

Women running their own businesses and volunteering is a symbiotic and natural association. Many communities are being revitalized because of personal and financial resources that volunteering women entrepreneurs invest.

An aspiring woman entrepreneur should seek out such volunteer mentoring organizations. There is almost always one or more of these groups in her community—groups like the *Wired Woman Society* dedicated to being of constructive, practical support in her quest for greater independence.

The Microloan

While many would-be businesswomen can't qualify for regular loans, they are increasingly finding funding from a fast-growing group of "microlenders" Inspired by banking in Third World nations, government agencies, non-profit organizations and a few banks are making very small loans a big business these days. The Small Business Administration classifies anything under $25,000 as a microloan. There are hundreds of new microlending institutions pumping millions into the economy. When an international social-policy organization looked at US microlending programs, it found that three out of four of the borrowers were women.

Microloans were conceived in Bangladesh, where small loans encouraged women to start their own enterprises. Loans as small as $10 were used to build craft and agriculture businesses. This led to the formation of Women's World Banking, a New York-based international lender that makes microloans in developing nations, enjoying almost 100% repayment rate. Demand is enormous.

The SBA provides funds to non-profit microlenders nationwide for low-interest loans, often with flexible collateral options.

Microloan Success Story

Some of microbanking's most dramatic success stories come from Bangladesh, where the Grameen Bank was founded over 20 years ago. Today, the Bank reaches into over 35,000 Bangladesh villages.[1]

A typical Grameen customer is Nurjahan, whose name means "the light of the world."

Abandoned at 3 months of age by her parents, Nurjahan was raised by a neighbor. Married at 12, she was then abandoned by her husband a year later when she was three months pregnant. She went to work as a cook for the family that had cared for her, and raised her son.

Until she joined the Grameen Bank, Nurjahan had never earned more than $35 - $40 a year. With access to loans of $100 - $200, five years later, she was making $250 a year (a bit more than the national average). At the time of writing she owns two goats, one pregnant cow, 10 chickens and two-thirds of an acre of land. Two farmhands hired on a seasonal basis help with her rice crop.

Perhaps most important, in a country where only 46% of children reach Grade 5, Nurjahan's son is in Grade 8.

The bank has over two million clients, 94% of them women. The average loan is about $100, with the repayment rates over 95%.

[1] *Globe and Mail*, Toronto, 6/27/98, p. 178, by Brian Milner.

9

Role Model Women Entrepreneurs

Global Link to Angels

"Sure we get women money. But the important thing we do is open doors."

Nina Brown
President and CEO
Women's Collateral World-wide Inc.
PO Box 166
Gladwyne, PA 19035

From a mainline Philadelphia background, Nina graduated from Bryn Mawr in the late 1980's. Then her marriage ended. She needed a job! No problem! But Nina never won a job she sought. A friend suggested she start a business. A business involving capital made sense to Nina — She knows people who have it. Nina developed a program for women business owners needing small loans, $5–25,000. Local business people said she would not be able to raise the venture capital because "nobody knows you." Shaken, Nina proposed an idea to Nick Jones, a successful local entrepreneur. Suppose she created a product to produce revenue, which in turn could be invested in women's businesses? Nick liked the idea. *The Women's Directory* was born, a publication of resources, advertising, and business advice.

The partnership between Nina and Nick grew into *Women's Collateral World-Wide Inc.*, to assist women who qualify for bank financing, but who have difficulty because they lack assets to pledge for loans. Nina and Nick purchase certificates of deposit as collateral for loans to women with good credit, sound plans and expertise. Nina and Nick receive 20-35% equity in the companies, and royalties. They have many success stories.

WCF no longer relies only on the Directory for funds, now often acting as a broker between loan clients and lenders. The SBA launched WCF as one of the first "Small Business Investment Companies" (SBIC) targeting women-owned businesses.

Nina's vision for WCF? She would like to "align with a global women's business network" to assist women entrepreneurs all over the world.

Creativity and Confidence

Linda Lundstrom
Linda Lundstrom Ltd.
33 Mallard Rd.
Toronto, Ontario
M3B 1S4

In 1974, with $10,000 borrowed from her parents and a belief in her own talent, Linda started her clothing design and manufacturing business.

Nearly twenty-five years later, *Linda Lundstrom Ltd.* is prospering; sales from a 37,000 square foot factory in Toronto continue their steady 12-15% annual growth. Five collections are produced per year, sold through some 500 American and Canadian boutiques on a cut-to-order basis.

For ten not-always-easy first years, Linda followed her "elusive dream," producing annual collections featuring stylish dresses and evening wear. Then during a trip to Japan, Linda was impressed with the importance of the traditional kimono on contemporary Japanese fashion.

Going back to her Canadian roots for inspiration, the result was a design focus on the parka, a traditional garment of the Canadian North.

Linda's two-layered "Laparka Concept" continues to be a selling phenomenon. A removable shell, water and wind resistant, acts as a year-round windbreaker. The inner wool jacket provides warmth, and can be worn on its own. The two layers combined, will resist almost any weather! Authentic native motifs adorn "Laparka" styles, reflecting Linda's commitment to enhancing awareness of native art and culture.

Born near Red Lake in remote Northern Ontario, where 75% of the population is First Nation, Linda developed a life-long fascination with native culture. The harsh Northern climate gave her an understanding of clothing for changing seasons.

The success of Linda's business is attributed not only to innovative product development, but also to its partnership approach to customers, suppliers and employees.

Company initiatives reflect Linda's commitment to native culture, e.g. all honoraria from Linda's numerous speaking engagements are donated to the "Kiishik Fund," supporting Native programs in the Red Lake District.

Linda believes… "investments in the health and well being of company people equip the company to meet future change."

Joyful Teaching

Kim Mitzo Thompson (right), Karen Mitzo Hildebrand
Twin Sisters Productions Inc.
D - 1340 Home Ave.
Akron, Ohio 44510

Twin Sisters Productions Inc. was started, in their 20's, by twin sisters Kim Mitzo Thompson, and Karen Mitzo Hildebrand.

Kim, with a Masters Degree in Curriculum Education, and Karen, with a degree in Industrial Engineering, share a love for music. Using her musical background in the classroom, Kim realized that students who had difficulty learning basic skills, found success when learning with music.

Kim and Karen wrote "Rap With the Facts," a rhythmic song to teach multiplication facts. Then realizing that "all students memorize their favorite songs in a manner of minutes," Kim and Karen decided to capitalize on this phenomenon—to use music to teach all basic skills.

In 1987, with $500 capital, Karen and Kim started Twin Sisters Productions Inc., a company to provide children with alternative ways to learn basic skills.

With a rapidly growing company, Kim left the teaching profession, and a year later Karen left engineering, both to commit full-time to the success of Twin Sisters Productions. Their company has since won major national awards for quality, age appropriateness and educational excellence.

Today the company has audio cassettes in Math, Foreign Language, Social Studies, Early Childhood, and Science. In addition the product line has branched out to include CD-ROM programs and Teacher Workbooks. These products are now sold to schools, bookstores, libraries and in direct mail catalogues.

Twin Sisters Productions Inc. donates money from every tape sold to the National Center for Missing and Exploited Children.

The success of Twin Sisters Productions results from Kim and Karen complementing each other's abilities. Kim focuses on product development and marketing opportunities; Karen on distribution, operations and sales.

Karen and Kim love what they do, love going to work each day. They share an adventurous spirit and a "We can do this" type of attitude, strong evidence that there's no one closer than a twin.

Service With Style

Sue McNair
Sooz Sewing Co.
Ganges
Salt Spring Island, BC
V8K 2L3

Sue McNair learned about free enterprise growing up in a family-owned fishing business. As the older sister of five brothers, she admits her "hard headedness and determination" came naturally. But, she also laughingly admits balancing her determination and hard headedness with the ability to "flutter" when the situation required it.

Sue's traditional upbringing with an at-home mother led her to believe that her life would follow suit. It wasn't until she became a single mother supporting three young children that she reversed her belief in her role as a woman. "Now, I had to become completely independent and self-reliant."

Knowing she would never be happy unless in business for herself, Sue first began manufacturing and selling children's clothing from her home. Visiting Salt Spring Island, Sue learned "Salt Spring needed a fabric store."

Within six weeks, Sue sold her mainland home, bought one on Salt Spring, moved herself and children into it, bought and renovated a store in a great location, stocked it, opened it... and started business.

After the first year, her accountant observed, "you're not making any money," to which Sue optimistically replied, "no, but I will,"—optimism made possible by the support of her family. "I knew they were there for me emotionally and financially, even if I didn't call on them."

Sue had no business plan but an absolute "blind faith" that she would succeed, "because I trust my gut instincts. I never buy or sell anything I don't love. I enjoy helping people, helping them create their own designs. A part of me goes into all their work."

Although Sue says, "her social life is at her store," she does recognize the importance of a balanced life, and her responsibility to her family. Sue probably works too hard, but she has learned to delegate responsibilities to co-workers who, above all else, "must have a similar philosophy of respect for our customers."

Sue summarized, "I'm not making a million dollars, but I am doing what I love and I am supporting my family. What else is there?"

Do What You Love

Erica Heyligers
Woodshine Finishing
127 Gold Road
Whitehorse
Yukon Territory
Y1A 2W4

Erica first became an entrepreneur in one of the classic ways. Because she is creative and loves working with wood, Erica secured a job as a full-time wood-worker. Six months later, in 1990, Erica had a chance to buy the business.

Erica went on to build *Woodshine Finishing* into a good business in Whitehorse, offering antique restoration, furniture repairs, refinishing, custom wood-working, and latterly, repairing musical instruments. Erica developed a steady clientele by being the only serious supplier of this expertise. Productive business relationships were also developed with moving and insurance companies.

Erica was able to obtain mentoring and support from the previous owner, a traditional source. She also receive emotional support from her family, and her father's line of credit was of important financial assistance.

Erica describes herself as being good at what she does, with flexible, varied creative abilities, and a dedication to doing what she loves to do. She comments that, "I think I have developed a personal relationship with my clients and they put a lot of faith in me."

Erica and her entrepreneurial woodworking success are now going through some lifestyle changes. Her woodworking business is for sale, because as this is written, Erica is expecting her first child. Her career focus has changed, too. Erica now wants to concentrate on the building and repair of guitars and has recently completed a seven-week course of instruction in that skill. Erica will now painstakingly and lovingly produce guitars, with delicate inlays, using abalone and other materials, not ever expecting or even wanting to make a fortune doing it.

As Erica says, "I like to work alone, to be dedicated, but I do not need to get bigger and richer."

She also observes, "I think sometimes it is an asset to be a woman entrepreneur because people tend to trust you more than men, especially if you show confidence in yourself."

Real Family Business

Marlene Wyatt
Wood Family Enterprises Inc.
PO Box 367
Yelleville, AK 72681

Wood Family Enterprises Inc. started as a pure, home-based, family-run enterprise. Marlene Wyatt, one of the founders explains, "I was always baking and needed something to make the clean-up and rolling out dough easier. So I took some material and put it over a board and this became the 'No Mess Dough Disc'."

Marlene (middle-left), sister Syble Whitlock (middle-right), niece Mona Elliott (left) and third sister, Pauline Dillard (right), now form the *Wood Family Enterprises Inc.*, and market the No Mess Dough Disc.

The No Mess Dough Disc package includes round plastic discs, a square plastic dough board, cloth covers for the discs, a cookbook and an apron.

For the first five years, the four women did everything themselves from their homes, and held down full-time jobs as well. Success did not come easily. In the beginning, instead of hiring a trucking firm to deliver the inventory, "we delivered it ourselves on a flatbed or pickup truck." They worked trade shows and fairs and "sometimes worked all night to get orders out." Today, partly as a result of winning a "QVC" electronic retailer "Quest for America's Best" contest, success appears assured. Over 230,000 Dough Discs have sold through QVC alone.

Wood Family Enterprises has recently moved out of their homes into a "church house" which they have remodeled into warehouse space. "We do our assembling in the pulpit and a large picture of The Lord's Supper hangs in the background." Marlene adds, "We thank the Lord and feel he has surely blessed us in so many ways."

Marlene, her sisters and niece admit they felt they were "taken advantage of because we were women." They agree, however, that as they learned more about the business world, they also learned to "be cautious, listen, and not to get in any hurry about making business decisions." They felt they were too trusting initially. If they could change anything, they would "do a lot more checking into the person or company before doing business."

Their advice to aspiring entrepreneurs: "If you have a plan and think it's worth doing, you should do it. But remember, nothing happens overnight. You have to be willing to work long, hard hours."

Dream... Hard Work... Beauty

Marcia Jeanne
Everlasting Summer
194 McLellan Dr.
Salt Spring Island, BC
V8K 1X2

Marcia Jeanne, owner of Salt Spring Island's *Everlasting Summer* gardening studio, enjoys following her heart. On an Asian trip at the end of her marriage, she studied botanical gardens and herbalist shops, knowing then her next step "…would come down to flowers." At art school later, on a part-time basis, Marcia grew, arranged and sold dried flowers.

Marcia found her dream portion of Salt Spring Island in 1983, when she first moved there to start a dried flower business. After four years Marcia acquired that dream… ten wooded and agricultural acres, a massive old barn, and a run-down one-bedroom house. Adding three adjoining acres, the 13-acre "Everlasting Summer" project was born.

With no business plan or sure salary, but knowing this is where she is meant to be, Marcia works tirelessly. She keeps a hands-on role with all work to clear land, design, build, plant, nurture and market Everlasting Summer's herbs and flowers. As Marcia says, she is a "mean hand with a tractor."

Marcia's business has grown substantially as the fame of Everlasting Summer and her creative products has spread. This gifted woman has a reputation in the Pacific Northwest for her magnificent garden, with its rainbow of high quality herbs, flowers and creative designs. This marvelous farm is now a must visit on tourist itineraries, and it is a site for school tours.

A direct-mail catalog features Marcia's dried flower and herb creations, plus related craft items from some of Salt Spring Island's renowned artisans. However, unless Marcia cloned herself, she knew she could produce only so many of her own hand-made items. This led to "Herbal Pantry of Salt Spring Island," a series of herbal and edible flower mixes for items like Rose Petal Cake, Lavender Glazed Cake, and Buttermilk Herb Soda Bread. Bulk-produced, Marcia does not need to give hands-on attention to every item. Working with an American partner, Marcia expects the Herbal Pantry of Salt Spring Island to help generate cash flow to finance more plans for the farm, such as a covered deck for weddings and other events.

What motivated her to be an entrepreneur? Marcia replies, "God knows… if I'd known… it took so much of me." But she is immensely proud when she has "touched someone… when they feel the magic I feel."

Perseverance and a Clear Niche

Eliza Minden
Gaynor Minden Inc.
140 West 16th St.
New York
NY 10011

Eliza Minden designed and developed her patented Gaynor Minden pointe shoe because "I saw a desperate need… from my own history in ballet. I also wanted to be my own boss, and I knew the glass ceiling would keep me down if I went the corporate route."

As a dancer, sister of a professional dancer and daughter of a dance teacher, Eliza grew up with family and friends all suffering sore toes from fragile pointe shoes. Eliza observed high-tech materials in athletic equipment and felt that pointe shoes could be improved using modern materials.

Although some of Eliza's friends and family "told me I was crazy and doomed to fail," her father "saw the wisdom of the product, and provided emotional, practical and financial support."

The introduction of the Gaynor Minden pointe shoe followed almost a decade of research and development. Creating this shoe proved far more complex than simply substituting a modern shank and toe box for the conventional cardboard, paste and burlap ones that had been standard since the turn of the century.

Drawing on the expertise of professional dancers, teachers and medical experts, hundreds of prototype shoes were tested—on different floors, in different climates, and on dancers with differing sizes, weights, abilities and foot types. When finished, Eliza knew she had a break-through product.

An important part of her research was consulting medical experts who specialized in the treatment of dancers. Doctors and physiotherapists now recommend Gaynor Minden pointe shoes to their patients. Eliza's plans include providing educational services on dancers' health and continuing to instruct students in dance history.

Today, Eliza and husband John, co-owners of a successful company, comment that, "Dancers are elite athletes as well as artists, and we provide dancers with superior products made from the best materials. We are happy to be considered revolutionary."

To aspiring women entrepreneurs, Eliza suggests, "Speak in a low voice. Understand that conversational styles and tactics that will earn you respect and acceptance from women are not always the same as those that will earn you respect from men. Always show respect for other people's skills, knowledge and experience."

Enterprising Home Health Care

Carolyn Colby
Spirit Home
Health Care
105 - 1000
Corporate Pointe
Culver City
CA 90230

Home health care is one of the fastest growing industries, as insurers, employers and consumers seek to cut health care costs. Carolyn's 10 year old firm, which provides patients in Los Angeles County with registered nurses, licensed practical nurses and home health aides, is taking advantage of this trend.

After three ownership changes of one of the nation's largest health care firms, of which Carolyn was a vice-president supervising 45 branches, Carolyn decided "to try it on her own." As she notes, "I'm black and I'm female—it would have been difficult to get a job of the same caliber—I didn't want to start at the bottom."

Despite experience, Carolyn, an RN with degrees in microbiology and health care administration plus an MBA, comments that: "I had no concept of how difficult it was to obtain capital—I started just as the recession hit, banks were starting to pull back. I went from bank to bank and they looked at me as though I was crazy—They wanted equity in a home. They wouldn't take receivables because the company was so new."

Short of bank collateral, Carolyn turned to factors. "Not only do they charge ridiculous rates of interest, but they hold a certain amount of your money in reserve all the time." Finally, in 1993, Carolyn secured a bank line of credit.

Now, with 50 full-time employees, many temporary employees and projected 1998 revenues of $3 million, the company is thriving.

Carolyn, who has won a CEO Award of the Year from her local chapter of NFWBO, has this advice for aspiring women entrepreneurs: "Don't give up until you have reached where you want to go. Make a business plan to decide how you are going to get there, then do it!"

Powerful Beliefs

Karen Buhlman and Patricia Hill
Interlude Romance Packages Ltd.
8898 Haro Park Trc.
Sidney, BC
V8L 4A2

Interlude Romance Packages Ltd. was created "because anyone can use more romance in their life, and more life in their romance." Karen, a young mother, and Patricia, Karen's mother, market "Romance Packages," elegant gift sets complementing romantic evenings, anniversaries, bridal showers, birthdays or other special occasions.

There are also packages for expectant or new mothers, even packages for those women who have spent their day gardening or golfing. Each package contains some combination of massage oil, bubble bath, body paints, candles, poetry, love coupons, and Karen's own "I love you because" cards. Pat and Karen ship packages all over the world.

In a moving speech at a recent women's event, Karen stated:

> I've long believed that women were the true source of strength for themselves and those around them. We've just had to be more subtle until now. I think that women as a group have realized that the traditional job market can't offer us financial independence. Traditional jobs are both under-utilizing our skills, and stifling our potential.
>
> It's not easy, learning that you have the right to put yourself first, and that you have the right to choose your own priorities. And it's not easy learning that you can create something special, and unique, and that, yes, you can become successful through your own efforts.
>
> But, not to try, to not take a chance, even once, I think, is to deny the ideals and dreams of those women who had the strength to forge ahead, to fight against prejudice, against sexism, to allow us the environment of freedom to do, and create, and strive and grow and blossom, and to become a personal success.

Rebuilding an Honorable Business

"Turnaround Success, Tough Woman—Tough Assignment, A Move to Success"

Marie Tomko
Pitman College
688 - 690
W. Hastings St.
Vancouver, BC
V6B 1P1

These Vancouver paper headlines introduce Marie Tomko's dream "to create the most exclusive private business college in BC."

Marie first joined Pitman College as a consultant and, in 1991, took charge of the old institution. In 1993, she became sole owner. Later, Marie received the Canadian Woman Entrepreneur of the Year Award in the Turnaround category; and in 1997 was given the Hall of Fame Award from the National Association of Career Colleges.

The college is celebrating its 100 year anniversary in 1998, and has a name that is "known forever." It had the stigma of being out of date, still teaching mostly typing and shorthand courses. To keep pace with the times, Marie moved the college to a new downtown Vancouver location and turned one floor of a stately old building into a state-of-the-art training facility. Enrollment has grown dramatically and now Pitman College operates at almost full capacity and boasting a graduate employment rate of over 90%.

Marie stresses customer service and a policy to "get the student working." Thus, students are taught skills needed for gainful employment, either retraining, or for entry level. "As the requirements of the job market change, we adapt" says Marie.

Marie fed her entrepreneurial spirit from early on, selling blackberries at age 9 to a local bakery. Marie states she came from "the wrong side of the tracks," but that probably helped her to develop the resilience she has needed since. She stresses that she and her business epitomize "quality and the ultimate in customer service." Classes are held year-round, and are flexible, with new start dates every month. Programs can even be custom-designed for students with specific areas of interest.

Marie's advice to fledgling women entrepreneurs is that there is (now) an abundance of help available. She believes that women should "go for it—chances are better than ever."

Courage... and a Business Plan

Gayle Arthur
Friends of the Family
77 Linsmore Cres.
Toronto, Ontario
M4J 4K2

In 1982, Gayle Arthur's marriage ended, she had a car accident, her mother died, and she was laid off from her job! She recovered from the first three, but concluded that "no one was going to offer me a job. If I wanted to work, I would have to create work for myself." She also decided that her work would have to be in a growth industry.

Gayle chose care for the elderly, beginning by providing Saturday night dinner, laundry, cleaning and shopping for an elderly gentleman. "Then neighbors asked if I could help them as well. Clearly there was a need."

Friends helped with the name, as the service provided "everything you would ask of a close friend of the family." They also encouraged Gayle with practical suggestions for marketing, promotion, etc. Her teenage children, working to support themselves while at school, were "enormously supportive and proud, and continue to be so."

Gayle worked 12–15 hour days, 7 days a week, developing the business. "I had no social life except Saturday morning breakfast with six or eight male friends who were encouraging and made me laugh." She did her books Saturday nights and "loved seeing numbers that showed I was growing.... After two years, I realized my business would survive."

Gayle's job rapidly evolved to that of employer and coordinator of services and marketing. She soon had three full-time office staff and a field staff of home support workers.

Though financing has been a constant struggle, Gayle is a believer that business plans are vital for helping to solve financial problems. Recently applying for a larger line of credit, Gayle spent six weeks revising her business plan. In the process, she sharply focused her thinking and planning not only for the current year, but for the next two as well.

In order to create a business, Gayle believes that you must have strong support from spouses, children, family and friends. Asked what she would change, Gayle says, "Nothing. I risked and achieved, and it was worth it."

She concludes, "Like successful men, women need supportive wives."

10

Your Business Plan

Guideline for Business Planning, Attracting Investors, and Applying for Business Loans

A business plan is probably the most important document involved in turning your business dream into reality. The business plan is a written summary of what you hope to accomplish, how you intend to do it and how you will measure progress. It is required to convince a lending officer or investor that you have thoroughly researched and planned your new business.

It may also be one of your toughest jobs. You may despair at the mountain of information needed. But think about it. Who really needs to have answers to questions? Who really is the beneficiary of a thorough business plan. Of course… it's you.

You will look and sound confident about your project, you will show that it is based on hard work, research, and knowledge, not just on enthusiasm.

Look upon the preparation of your business plan positively. Enjoy the reward of finding sound answers to tough questions. With the proper preparation, you will dramatically increase your chances for success.

Why Prepare a Plan

- It encourages realism.
- It helps identify customers, market area, pricing strategy and competitive conditions.
- It can lead to discovery of new opportunities, as well as exposing deficiencies in your plan.
- By committing plans to paper, your tools for managing the business and anticipating problems will increase.
- A well-organized plan makes it easier to assess your proposal, and you.
- Some hours spent each month updating your plan will save you time and money in the long run and may even save your business.

> *I often think women are better investors than men. They are more patient and not so inclined to think they have great insight.*
>
> – Steve Bareham, The Globe and Mail, Toronto, 3/7/98

Recommended Format

The business plan format, introduced below, and outlined in detail commencing page 204, is a starting point for organizing your own plan.

Executive Summary

The format should start with an Executive Summary, including your mission statement. A crisp, one or two-page introduction helps capture attention.

Part I — Business Concept

Part I identifies market potential within your industry. The heart of the business concept is your monthly sales forecast for the coming year. It is a statement of confidence in your marketing strategy and forms the basis for cash flow and projected income.

Part I also contains an assessment of business risks and a contingency plan. Be open about your risks and how you plan to deal with them. This is realistic management thinking.

Part II — Financial Plan

This outlines present financing and identifies financing sought. Be concise, with supporting material supplied only when requested. The financial plan contains forecasts, called "pro formas." These forecasts are your guide to business survival and profitability. Refer to them often. Keep them current.

Before presenting your plan, review it with your advisors. This will improve both theirs and your understanding of what the statements reveal about your business.

Part III — Cash Flow Forecast

A cash flow is a periodic forecast. It is not a pro-forma income statement. A cash flow is not an estimate of sales and expenses; it is an estimate of when money will be received and when money for expenses will be available—see Cash Flow Forecast information commencing on page 209.

The body of the plan will describe highlights of each topic, with support documents in an appendix. In the appendix, include documents such as personal tax returns, cash flow forecasts, financial statements, debt/equity structure, references, product/service literature, surveys, management biographies. Make the final package attractive and professional looking.

11

Some Strong Strategies

Support Systems

> **Love Yourself Too**
>
> Re-read old cards or nice letters from family and friends, newspaper clippings you are proud of, any other commendations. Post them where you can see them. Remind yourself of how clever, accomplished, and brave you are… and how loved.

All business owners need support networks of family, friends, co-workers, business and social acquaintances to provide information, and advice. Women business owners often need those support systems even more than men because they usually still hold primary responsibility for home and family, and can feel torn by the conflicting demands.

The greatest source of support may well be the family. Be sure this network knows it is needed; be sure that members have access and are welcome.

A mentor is also one of the key people you need to know and trust in your support system. An ideal mentor knows something about your business, and will act as a sounding board.

Formal networks are business associations. Informal networks can be community organizations… service clubs, church and recreational groups. Both provide for meeting people, finding customers, employees, suppliers, advisors and mentors.

Arranging for Child Care

Though obvious, this is often a key consideration and not always easy to solve. The first place to look for child care, often overlooked, is among family. For instance, how flexible can your spouse be? Can you dovetail schedules to take care of a portion of day-caring needs? How about grandparents? Neighbors? Other parents?

> *Imagine what we could accomplish if we did not care who got the credit.*
>
> – Unknown

Other sources for child care include community organizations and Public Health Offices. The most effective source is recommendations from friends or co-workers. The checklist on page 212 will help you rate the child care facilities in your area.

The following quote is not directly about business, but it does remind us all of some fundamentals:

> "Raising healthy children is a labor-intensive operation. Contrary to the news from the broader culture, most of what children need, money cannot buy. Children need time and space, attention, affection, guidance and conversation. They need sheltered places where they can be safe as they learn what they need to know to survive. They need jokes, play and touching. They need to have stories told to them by adults who know and love them in all their particularity and who have a real interest in their moral development.
>
> In the current family-hurting culture, families must do two things to survive: They must protect themselves from what is most hurtful to the health of the family and they must connect with what is good outside the family. These tasks require time and energy, both of which are scarce commodities in an era when many parents work long hours at jobs far from their homes.
>
> Remember, the "family" can be traditional families with parents and children, extended families which include grandparents, aunts, uncles and cousins, or "formed" families of close friends who share ideas and beliefs, as well as meals and activities.
>
> Hopefully these various kinds of families are each realizing the common goal to give children back childhood with safe spaces, protected time, good nourishing information and lessons on how to behave." [1]

---

[1] Excerpted from: *In The Shelter of Each Other*, Mary Pipher, Ballantine, 1997, p.221.

Dealing with Stress

> **For Stress Relief:**
>
> Take three deep breaths. Then take a break. If you can yawn, you'll completely release tension.

Stress takes many forms: physical illness, lack of concentration, procrastination, mood swings, crying, irritability, headaches, ulcers, even heart attacks. Dealing with stress can be stated simply. Learn how to delegate, find ways to laugh at your problems, learn yoga, take a vacation—or all of the above, and more!

But whatever your strategy, good time management is essential… to complete work, be with friends and family, to do things you enjoy… and reduce stress. The checklist on page 212 will help you determine your status as a "Time Manager."

> *Ask yourself, "What simple activities restore the gentleness of my spirit?"*
>
> – Linda Kavelin Popov, "Sacred Moments: Daily Meditations on The Virtues."

Review the Health of your Business Frequently

Regular reviews need to include analyses of costs, receivables, payables, forecasts vs actuals, statements of profit and loss and balance sheet, assessments of staff performance… and of your own performance.

- Once a year, do a formal review of actual against planned performance. Did you achieve your goals? Update your business plan.
- Prepare a summary of conclusions and changes you plan to make in the next year.
- Obtain advice regularly from industry experts, business mentor, your outside board.

Discuss this information with your financial institution. Pay attention to early warning signs such as loss of customers, increasing costs, inventory piling up, overdue accounts receivable, results that differ from forecasts.

Tap the Power of Computers

It is not essential that you do your financial analyses long-hand, or laboriously typed. Doing number-crunching by computer will be so much easier and faster that you may actually **do** it almost as often as you should!

Your accountants will help you set up your control and reporting systems—with programs they know will meet your needs. Some 9 out of 10 women-owned firms use computers, both for the tasks mentioned above and for a wide range of other purposes.

> *Adversity is often opportunity in disguise.*
>
> – Unknown

12

Management By Common Sense

Management

Model Employers Provide:

1. A genuine caring attitude
2. Open, informal communication
3. Honesty and integrity
4. Performance feedback
5. Opportunity for development
6. Proper training
7. Tailored benefits and incentives
8. A sense of teamwork
9. A defined mission
10. Well-conceived systems

There is enormous literature on management available for study, so comments here are limited to a few universal truths, applicable by any supervisor in almost any situation.

Much of management is simply dealing with people as you like to be dealt with.

Good managers no longer just give orders. They consult with and ask the advice of equals, i.e. the people doing the work. Most employees respond better if they share in the decision-making process. Managers who don't recognize this, and who rely on old fashioned militaristic ways will not be as successful as those who use the consultative process.

Women are in the forefront of special programs which empower and inspire employees, and which encourage teamwork. Women entrepreneurs often structure their companies around social agendas for which they have conviction. New attitudes of care and concern about communities and the earth proliferate among women entrepreneurs. Women are creating companies that employees are happy to join.

While encouraging participation, sharing power and working to enhance the self-worth of co-workers, as owner/manager you do have to prove you know your stuff! And also that "pleases" and "thank-yous" aren't indications of weakness. In some traditional male fields, there may be attempts to bully or buffalo you. Such attitudes are much less common today. Just remember Zsa Zsa Gabor's observation, "Macho does not prove mucho."

However, any owner/manager is well-advised to understand the work situations, to pay attention and ask lots of questions. Never be afraid to accept sound advice! Try to attend management courses so you can evaluate your own styles and study working effectively with employees and other managers.

Ultimately, managers must make decisions. But if the process has been fair and involving for those affected, and information is shared with all employees, this is no longer as formidable as it once was. After all, most people want to do their job and do it right. They need clear pictures, which emerge from well reached decisions.

Most managers today have little patience with the idea that men won't take direction or criticism from a woman. Anyone can handle criticism or take direction if it's done constructively. The matter gets talked over, ways to improve are both solicited and suggested. This lets the employee know that both you and they know they can do better. Wonderful results occur when information is shared among employees who then run with the information, and later, challenge management. Good management means doing your homework, listening to employees and seeking to motivate rather than just giving orders. Gender becomes quite immaterial.

> **Staff Disputes**
>
> The first thing quarreling employees must be made to realize is that it's their responsibility to solve a problem, never mind who is to blame. When this responsibility is accepted, the largest step forward to solving the problem has been taken.

Negotiation

Negotiation is different. Being good at building relationships and getting consensus works well in management, where creativity and cooperation create positions that keep both sides in a discussion.

But negotiations can be uncomfortable and adversarial situations. It's often difficult to make friends, and to be effective in situations where you want to make the best deal for yourself. Preparation is your most powerful tool. Prepare in detail what you wish in an agreement, identifying your best alternatives. Preparation includes research on the other party. In order to reach a great deal for yourself, you must also know what your adversary's needs are. By making inquiries among suppliers, bankers, accountants, etc., you may learn about the real agenda of the other side. Thorough preparation may enable you to steer the process into consensus building.

Silence is often a valuable tool. Don't think you must jump in when things get quiet. Let silence cause the other side to offer more information, or at least feel compelled to speak. Surprising things happen.

A creative mentor playing the devil should walk you through the preparation for negotiations, rehearsing you.

Making Decisions

Never easy. Fraught with risk. But essential. Decisions must be made and procrastination doesn't help. Here are questions which may be useful when you simply must make a timely decision:

- What is the real issue?
- Do I have all the information?
- Do I decide this alone?
  If not, who else inside or outside the firm shall I involve?
- Must I decide now?
- Are any lessons from the past helpful here?
- Who may be hurt?
- To whom, how and by when do I need to deliver an unambiguous decision?
- Is there a workable compromise, or a safety net?
- Are the governing rules still appropriate?
- What lessons are there for all in this situation?
- D.I.R.M. (Does It Really Matter?)

Remember that one valid management option is to do nothing, providing you reach that decision logically and deliberately, not just because it may be easy. Often, what seems to be a problem just goes away, or solves itself.

It takes two to speak truth. One to talk, one to hear. – Anonymous

Hiring

Interviewing job candidates is a difficult task. Common mistakes include:

- **Talking too much.** Entrepreneurs often dominate interviews, talking about their company and not listening to the candidate. The interviewee should do the talking, with the interviewer providing only basic information about the company and the position.
- **Not taking notes.** Early candidates in an interviewing session are often forgotten. Notes, and sometimes even photos, are essential if many candidates are being considered.
- **Getting off track.** Too often, interviews wander into conversations about unrelated topics which interest both parties. Using a list of questions will minimize this.

Danger Signals

An entrepreneur is often so glad for assistance that she may overlook the possibility that her "irreplaceable" assistant is actually a smooth cheat! Whatever your business, these danger signs can alert you to an employee who may be embezzling funds:

- Rewriting records for the sake of "neatness"
- Refusing vacations; never taking personal or sick days
- Working overtime excessively; refusing to release custody of records during the day
- Unusually high standard of living considering salary
- Gambling in any form, beyond believable ability to withstand losses
- Refusal of promotion
- Replying to questions with unreasonable explanations
- Getting annoyed at reasonable questions
- Inclination toward covering up inefficiencies and mistakes
- Pronounced criticism of others (to divert suspicion)
- Frequent association with members of a supplier's staff
- Excessive drinking or associating with questionable characters.

Intuition

Intuition, gut feelings, an inner voice—these describe the phenomenon of the spontaneous and urgent thought which tells you that something makes sense, or that it does not. Some people ignore it, some do the opposite!

Intuition is a constructive decision-making resource. The inner voice is guided by past experience; intuitive thoughts do not occur out of the blue. The trick is to balance intuition with patience, then logic.

Planning, establishing goals, managing change are all areas where intuition is useful, because these tasks deal with the intangible and the unknown.

Making decisions about people often calls upon intuition—about personality and chemistry; factors revealed more by gut reactions than in a résumé. This does not mean abandoning logic, research and deduction input from others. Analysis and evaluation are still essential.

First, ask yourself what assumptions your feelings are based on. Have colleagues challenge these assumptions. Challenge them yourself; sleep on them. Tuning in to your inner mind is not easy. You need to be able to talk to it, and listen to it. A strong self-image is also important. If you lack confidence in yourself, you won't listen to the inner voice.

As an entrepreneur, you are in charge of every decision. You have the authority to stretch your intuition to its maximum. So, when next faced with a major decision, let your intuition go to work, too. It is a prime way to use your mind. Don't let intuition go to waste.

Repair Mistakes — Now!

Most unhappy customers will not complain directly about discourteous treatment, but almost all of them will be lost forever. Further, every one of those unhappy customers will share their experiences with others.

So drill into yourself and staff the following strategies:

- The customer *is* always right. Get a complete story of the customer's problem, resolve it to the customer's satisfaction and be flexible doing so.
- Honesty *is* the only policy. Acknowledging mistakes is vital to retaining customer confidence and goodwill.
- An apology is *always* in order.
- Empower every employee to resolve customer problems. Encourage them to seek help from more senior employees.
- Since no one is perfect, minimize finger-pointing. Use the incident as a learning tool.
- Act now! Don't jeopardize rapport with that customer by delay.
- Get customer feedback. Keep getting it—"Is everything okay **today**?"

Filing Systems

While not as dramatic as other topics, a system of filing the paper your business will generate ranks high on the scale of management needs. Start with the main categories, e.g. Administration, Communications etc., and build your filing system as you need it.

A guide to an excellent filing system is found on page 213.

Got a Complaint?

- Stay cool. Start by contacting the company. Be sure to have complete documentation about model, warranty, sales receipt, etc., or all details about a service contract.
- Record who you talk to, keep careful notes, note how many calls you've had to make.
- Know your rights. Call the nearest agency that handles your kind of problem. Ask to speak to legal counsel, request copies of relevant laws. Ask whether you can send copies of correspondence to them.
- Be ready to escalate. Say who you are going to contact next—regulatory agencies, local media, state consumer protection agencies, etc.

Insurance

Be honest with your insurance agent. Get good advice by giving complete information. There is no point paying money only to find out your insurance is void because of some restriction. The goal is for you and the agent to come up with insurance that gives you and your business necessary protection for:

- house/business premises
- vehicle
- liability
- business interruption
- disability
- partnership
- product or service

Guard Against Insurance Fraud

Call your regional insurance department before you buy any policy to verify that the insurer exists and the agent is authorized by that company. Always make out the check to the company, not the agent. Be sure the policy is delivered to you, not kept by the agent. If you have any doubts, return the policy within 10 days after receiving it; expect a full refund.

Taxation

You need your accountant to guide you through the minefields of taxation, a task not to be tried here! Some useful general concepts follow, but remember… **talk to your accountant!**

According to income tax law, all money you spend "…for the purpose of gaining or producing income" can be deducted from your business and employment income. If you work out of your home, you can deduct a portion of your overhead expenses such as: telephone; rent, lease or mortgage payments; a portion of vehicle expenses; office equipment; furniture and supplies; business stationery and relevant books. Depreciation rates on equipment differ for various categories of equipment.

Some possible ways to reduce business income taxes include:

- If you are based at home, claim the expenses of the physical space you use.
- Claim pay phone and parking meters. Use your daily calendar to record expenses for which you have no receipts. Transfer this record onto your monthly petty cash sheet, marking which are paid by cash and especially noting cash expenses that have no receipt. Without that habit, cash will dribble through your fingers without being recorded as business expenses. The ones paid by check will show up as a business expense in your check book.
- Organize receipts in envelopes, then transfer amounts to financial records. If you lose receipts, legitimate business expenses can still be deducted. Note the expense in your appointment book and include with other receipts an explanation of expenses claimed but not supported by receipts.
- Collect gasoline and repair receipts to claim "use for business" expenses.
- Keep a list of business assets and their costs; make sure you deduct capital cost allowance in tax calculations.

Management Thoughts

Action – Analyze, evaluate, then act. Make the decision!
Service – Always first priority; good quality should be a given.
Trust – Develop terms of reference, then let your teams proceed.
Independence – Let employees experiment, innovate. Tolerate mistakes!
Customers – Top service to current customers attracts new ones.
Learn – Today's technology is already old. Learn about tomorrow's.
Listen – To suppliers, customers, employees. Let them teach you.
Cost Control – It is essential, but never at the cost of quality.
Growth – Slow and steady, assures learning, improving—and lasting!

Reading

One of your major responsibilities as owner-manager, to yourself, investors and employees, is to be up to date on developments in your type of business. This includes not only technology or research or new products etc., but also a sense of broader social shifts influencing day-to-day life.

This refers to such events as corporate mergers, technological advances, downsizing, production re-located overseas, contracting out, temporary employees, etc. These shifts also include health and nutrition, recreation, environmental concerns, etc. All of these events are producing profound changes in North America's traditional career, job, employment and living patterns. These in turn are influencing the development and growth of new entrepreneurial niches.

From time to time, seminal books are published on the above types of subjects. Such books are informative and thought provoking. Set out on page 216 is a partial list of such books, books that have been on my bedside table recently. My list is obviously not exhaustive!

Sometimes one also stumbles across passages in novels which are touchingly relevant to your own ideas. For me, one such extraordinary passage occurs in *The Dossier*,[1] a novel published back in 1984, as follows:

> "...there is something else," she said. "It has to do with the future, with women, and how they'll change the country, and what women will do to the thinking process of the country. In the past what women have thought and felt never counted for much. Now it counts, believe me, and even more important, women **value** what they think and feel. And what they think and feel **is** different from what men think and feel. They're **not** as aggressive. They absolutely detest wars because they carried the people who fought them. Women **are** more sensitive and caring and humane. They **do** have a more sensitive emotional register, which means that they are more aware of others thoughts and feelings. When the values that women carry come more and more to influence their sons, then the sons are going to change. They won't be so aggressive. They won't like war so much. They'll be more sensitive and caring and humane and maybe a little less competitive. Then America may have a chance to become the kind of place you envisioned."

---

[1] Pierre Salinger & Leonard Gross, Doubleday, 1984, pp. 213-214.

13

Role Model Women Entrepreneurs

Helpful Hands

Michelle Fanto-Chan (l),
President
Denise O'Brien (r),
Partner
Rocky Mountain
Moms Inc.
28591 Golden
Gate Canyon Rd.
Golden, Colorado

"Rocky Mountain Baby Inc." is a business with a "mother-invented children's product line" designed by Denver partners Michelle and Denise. These products were created "as a departure from the typical baby products conceived by industrial designers and marketing executives." After trials and errors, frustrations and successes, these "mothers of invention" products are guaranteed to work.

Rocky Mountain Baby Inc. markets nine products through various catalogs, department stores and specialty shops around the country. Products include unique designs, such as a wrap-around baby "Hugster," a special nursing pillow, and the "Shady Baby," a baby seat insert with a detachable sun bonnet.

Not content with marketing their own products, these generous and concerned women also run *Rocky Mountain Moms Inc.*, a company whose mission is to assist other women entrepreneurs. The impetus for this was the direct result of Michelle and Denise's own struggles and experiences of selling, licensing and bringing to market their Rocky Mountain Baby products.

Rocky Mountain Moms Inc. supplies an "inventor's package" containing information on marketing, patents, trademarks, licensing, financing and running a business.

Michelle, like many other successful woman/mother entrepreneurs, sees delegating as a problem, but an essential management skill. She says she has to remind herself to "take time to enjoy life now."

1998 Update: Denise has returned to teaching and is now a silent partner, although she and Michelle still work together on product design.

Networking... And Service

Jennifer Arsenault
Jennifer's New Home Service
1227 48th Ave. NW
Calgary, Alberta
T2K 0Z6

Jennifer is one home-based entrepreneur seldom at home. She is usually out in the field checking the work of her clients. In 1990, with the confidence of 25 years' construction industry experience behind her, Jennifer got herself a desk, a phone, a computer, and started providing the then only after-sales, warranty-satisfaction-service for Calgary builders. Visiting the buyer who has taken possession of the new home from the builder, Jennifer accompanies that home buyer on a methodical and thorough inspection of the quality and finish of the home.

Then, based on the specific warranty from that home buyer's builder, and from detailed inspection notes, Jennifer arranges for professional trades to come to the home and complete any necessary work to the buyer's satisfaction. This is an invaluable service both to the home buyer and to the builder. The builder does not have to maintain a service department, and the home buyer is guaranteed good-quality work based on clear warranty criteria.

Jennifer tried working in an office away from home, but soon returned to her basement home office. She felt her business would develop better from home, and make it easier for her to give her customers 24-hour seven-days-a-week service. Jennifer has developed a fine reputation for reliability, quality and service.

As a benefit of considerable publicity, Jennifer recently started a new company called "CLJ Software Corporation" to market "U-Track," the software for the deficiency monitoring program. This is the same program that enables her to give good service to her three client groups: the trades, the home buyers and the builders.

A strong believer in networking, Jennifer is active in several builder and civic association. As she says, "every single person I have ever been in contact with, I contact them again."

Determined Faith

Gail Bryn-Jones
Virtues Project Facilitator
Ganges
Salt Spring Island, BC
V8K 2L3

Gail decided to follow her heart and her intuition. This mother of two, secure in the teaching profession, put that on hold to make her living teaching *The Virtues Project*, introduced on page 155 in the article about Linda Kavelin Popov. Gail is doing it from a conviction about the fundamental worth of the project, rather than relying on it for a major income. "It is about sharing concepts and serving humanity."

Gail assisted in the seminal development of *The Virtues Project* in 1990, by helping to edit the first edition of *The Virtues Guide.* She also attended the first "Virtues Project Facilitator Training" in 1991, conducted by founders Linda Kavelin Popov and husband, Dr. Dan Popov. Since then, Gail has presented many Virtues workshops in British Columbia, and in New Zealand while on a sabbatical there with her family.

There are few criteria for Gail's venture. A business plan would change daily; cash-flow projecting is tenuous. A strong conviction is Gail's chief resource. "I just know this is the most important thing I can be doing right now, and as long as I am faithful to the integrity of the Project, I know it will take me to places I haven't yet dreamed about." Her partner, Martin, supports Gail's need to pursue her vision.

In 1997 Gail's presentations included one at the annual "Wellness Conference" in Vancouver, British Columbia, and a Virtues based healing retreat for the Saddle Lake First Nations Counseling Services in Alberta. Gail's objectives include becoming a trainer of facilitators, being a quality control consultant, and eventually, a global trainer of trainers.

I know and love this young woman, my daughter and mother of Helena and Arlo, two of the children to whom this book is dedicated. It is rewarding to observe the security and ease with which these young children have responded to the language, and now practice the values of The Virtues.

As Gail observes: "By helping parents learn ways to raise the self-esteem of their children, I believe I am doing a service which will help lead to world peace and unity."

Reverence for Nature

Chris Czajkowski
Nuk Tessli
Alpine Experience
Nimpo Lake, BC
V0L 1R0

To get away, consider Chris Czajkowski's wilderness center. In British Columbia, from Williams Lake, drive 200 miles west to Nimpo Lake. Then, hike into Chris' haven taking two to three days, if you are experienced. Or, fly in by chartered float plane. Once there, be on your own, or be part of a guided group, endearingly described by Chris as "…the putterers," who enjoy not-too-strenuous guided hikes. Seasoned back-country skiers can access serious alpine country where they are not likely to see another soul!

In the late 1980's, a loner wanting "a life in the bush," Chris needed a commercial reason to get permission to lease government land to develop Nuk Tessli. Naturalist-type tourism best fitted as a complying business.

Chris then built the facilities herself, single-handedly, of resources from her property. Using chain-saws, peaveys, come-alongs and gin poles, Chris hauled trees lakeside, peeled and milled them, measured, trimmed and fitted them, to construct rugged accommodations. With supplies and tools arriving by floatplane, weather permitting, Chris worked alone, with only dogs as companions, contending with tough terrain, bears, minus 40° temperatures, and needing snowshoes for any winter travel… including to her outhouse.

This remarkable story is detailed in Chris' *Diary of a Wilderness Dweller*, 1996, Orca Press. See entry for 8/22/88… "I have a bear in camp in broad daylight and I am in a blue panic about it… because of my broken glasses everything [is] blurry…" She also reverently and lovingly describes her magnificent, lonely, mountain country, and the rugged people who live there, stressing the crucial sense of responsibility they feel for one another.

In England, Chris earned an agricultural degree, then taught in Uganda. Later, she traveled through Asia, South America, the South Pacific, finishing up in New Zealand where she learned mountaineering and cabin building.

Money always a problem, Chris has always found friends "who will feed me or trade for work or art when funds are low." To supplement income in early days at Nimpo Lake, Chris went tree-planting each spring. Now, her wilderness business growing, and with book, painting and lecture revenues, life is a little easier, though she "never expected to make much money at it." As Chris says, "it's a lifestyle… it allows me to be where I want to be… to enjoy what I want to do… I also know who I am."

Enthusiastic Confidence

Jennie Avram
Station Events Inc.
42 - 2231 Albert St.
Regina, Saskatchewan
S4P 2Y6

With a background in Event Management that enabled her confidently to offer, "the best customer service in the city," Jennie Avram set up Station Events Inc. in 1993.

Jennie intuitively knew that "to have exclusive use of the most spectacular historical building in the province would attract business."

Jennie's business offered the special setting of a classic, romantic and nostalgic old railway station, as "a unique alternative to the conventional hotel and convention facilities available" for weddings, concerts, banquets and other special events.

For her initiative, at age 28, Jennie won the 1994 Federal Business Development Bank Young Entrepreneur Award.

Since that time, the old station has been converted to other uses by the government owners and Jennie had to regroup and diversify her efforts. She now works out of her home and has converted Station Events into a consulting firm offering marketing, communications and fundraising expertise.

The business has done very well... "thanks to my creative background and keen attention to detail, I believe I bring fresh and innovative approaches to solving my customers' problems." Jennie is proud of the company's growth. "If you don't keep growing you lose momentum and fade quickly."

Jennie credits her strong spiritual faith, unwavering principles, and a solid customer service ethic to the success of Station Events. These philosophies have helped her earn and maintain the respect of her customers.

"Business associates and mentors are my greatest assets when I encounter a problem... we all need someone to bounce ideas off. It is imperative to have support close by, especially when you're a one person operation."

Honesty, Courage... and Resilience

Scott Shuhany
Scott's Kids
87 Georges Cres. NW
Edmonton, Alberta
T2N 3M7

"I had the creative ideas and was tired of giving them to others. I wanted to try a business of my own." So began in 1987 Scott's Shuhany's home-based clothing design company. She spent the next six years concentrating her efforts on Canadian and American retailers. Her line of upscale children's clothing, for "the grandparents market," was picked up by such retail giants as Breton's in Canada, and Macy's in the United States.

During these early years, she was a one woman show with tremendous financial and practical help from her family: "Mother who sewed on the buttons and snaps, an involved father, and a husband who was a CA." Scott's success was due to her confidence in her designs, high quality products, and years and years of determination.

After six years, a great distance from suppliers and manufacturers, facing the slow-pay pattern of some retailers, Scott dropped the wholesale end of the business and moved back into her home. She changed to direct mail and produced two catalogs featuring her high-quality children's clothing.

This proved to be another "learning experience" for Scott. Success in retailing did not guarantee success in direct mail. After eight years in business, Scott simply burned herself out. "I was far too busy for any social interaction; all the money we made went back into the business… there was little salary for me… I haven't golfed in seven years… we stopped manufacturing… now I just sell to friends and supply one local store."

Particular thanks are due to Scott for so openly sharing her experiences.

Presently "regrouping," taking time to reflect and to evaluate her whole business strategy, Scott candidly admits, "next time, I'll be an entrepreneur with a balanced life."

Scott Shuhany is an honest, inspiring woman who "loved being an entrepreneur." You believe her when she states, "You will be hearing from me."

Seizing a Niche

Nicola Perry
Tea and Sympathy
108 Greenwich Ave.
New York, NY
10011

To be virtually first in a niche in the restaurant business in a market like New York is a fine achievement on its own. To have your establishment visited and blessed by celebrities is to obtain approval and publicity you just cannot buy.

Such is the situation for the evocatively named "Tea and Sympathy" founded by Nicola Perry in 1991 as the first "British" restaurant in New York City's Greenwich Village. A transplant from London, "Nikki" worked in New York restaurants for a number of years, nurturing the dream of having her own establishment.

Nikki was confident that she had not only a great idea, but also "loads" of experience. So, with determination that says, "It's done my way—[I] don't put up with bad attitude from anyone," Nikki collaborated with her father for some financing, her brother for design and rebuilding, and proceeded to make her dream real.

Nikki describes her operation as a "cross between a classic British teashop and a restaurant with a bit of pub atmosphere." It is cozy, with ten tables, and a very British menu—Bangers and mash, shepherd's pie, Welsh rarebit, sardines on toast, steak and mushroom pie, etc., plus a lavish selection of desserts. All reviews agree the food is excellent.

Mixing London charm with strict attention to good food and service, Nikki has made her restaurant a haven. Regulars are greeted endearingly, "sit down and be quiet, love." As members of the "tea club," they get their tea free. With infectious and unfailing bonhomie, Nikki strikes up conversations with all who enter.

Nikki wanted "to show Americans that English food is good, and all this nonsense about British food written here in the States is rubbish."

Unique Products

Paula Lishman
Paula Lishman Ltd.
Box 280
Blackstock, Ontario
L0B 1B0

Paula Lishman drew on Labrador roots to create a process for knitting fur and cotton into unique garments offering high fashion on the outside and warmth on the inside. She has developed her business globally since its founding in 1979. In 1995, Paula won the Canadian Entrepreneur of the Year Award for International Competitiveness. She credits success to awareness of fashion trends and the ability to design for distinct markets.

Believing from the beginning in exports for her success, Paula notes that "exports to the US, Japan and Europe now account for 80% of the business." She knew Japan was likely the "most demanding market in the world… requiring high standards of excellence… my line was perfected there."

Paula works primarily with beaver, a species abundant in Canada. She points out that overpopulation of the animal in some areas has contributed to environmental problems such as flooding and soil erosion. She adds that fur is a natural biodegradable product, while synthetic fabrics are not.

Paula has grown an internationally competitive company while maintaining simple cottage-industry roots at home. Part of the production takes place in a 100 year old school house in Blackstock, Ontario and well as in industrial units in a nearby town. The remainder is done by 160 women who work out of their homes, knitting, cutting and finishing the fabrics, much the same as Paula did in the beginning.

In keeping with her desire to tread lightly on this planet, Paula's plans for her business are to build an "earth friendly" factory, keeping the whole company "under one roof and not spread out, in a co-operative space utilizing a Living System work technology." This concept is an extension of the "earth-house" in which she lives with her three children and husband Bill. Bill Lishman is internationally known as "Father Goose" for his development of new migratory routes for endangered water fowl… and for key input into the wonderful movie about Canada Geese called "Fly Away Home"

Paula is an entrepreneur who feels strongly about promoting and exporting by Canadian businesses. She suggests that "if Canadians want to be economically successful, they need to add creativity and workmanship to their products, to sell finished goods rather than raw materials."

Strong Niche... Great Success

Val Middleton (l) and
Roz Isaac (r)
Midlyn Advertising Inc.
PO Box 86097
North Vancouver, BC
V7L 4J5

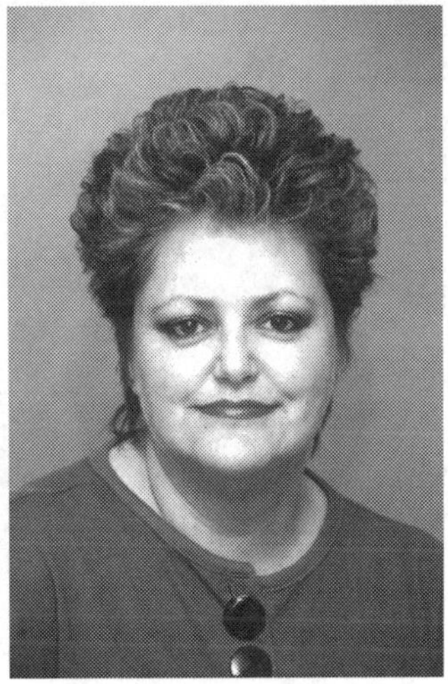

Sisters and partners, Val Middleton and Roz Isaac have together built a very successful, fully accredited advertising agency in Vancouver, British Columbia, specializing in recruitment advertising.

As a pioneer in recruitment advertising in Cape Town, South Africa, Val has 20 years' experience in this industry. With in-depth knowledge of all aspects of the business, it was a natural step for Val to start Midlyn Advertising in Vancouver, BC in 1990 when she emigrated to Canada.

Joined by her sister, Roz, who also has senior international recruitment advertising experience, Val and Roz have truly complemented each other's skills. Val calls herself the consummate networker and the builder of "a great team which goes the extra mile" for its clients. Roz concentrates more on actual client management, discerning client needs and employing the team to meet them.

In 1994, Val and Roz won the BC New Canadian Entrepreneur of the Year Award. Then in 1995, Val won the prestigious Start-Up Category in British Columbia of the Canadian Woman Entrepreneur of the Year Awards.

Would Val do it again? Of course. But now knowing that she would encounter not only normal resistance to obtaining financing, but additional resistance being an immigrant from South Africa, she would "be far more aggressive."

Realizing how successful Val and Roz have been already, one blanches a little, then smiles, at the thought of "more aggressive." But as Val counsels prospective woman entrepreneurs, "if you have a good idea, take the opportunity to become an entrepreneur, work hard and never give up."

User Friendly

Anne Lambert
Science Connection Inc.
PO Box 599
Chester, Nova Scotia
B0J 1J0

Noting networks for single people with special interests, such as books, classical music etc, Anne reasoned that there was an opportunity for a singles meeting service for people with interests in Science and Natural History.

Anne established Science Connection Inc., a membership organization that functions as a social network for science professionals and devotees. Members receive information on all members in an initial mailing, and monthly updates. They then contact each other directly. "We try for a dignified and civil tone in our advertising and information material."

Anne, a biologist formerly working in wildlife research and bird studies, wanted something more secure than working on contracts. She also wanted to get away from the city, to live in a small community in an area that she liked. Like many of her friends, Anne had been thinking up possible business ideas all her working life. "Science Connection was the first one I tried, although I seriously considered and researched going into garlic farming."

Anne reports "...business is steady... could be better. But we have felt the need to produce an electronic, on-line component of the network... and we now have a Web page for that purpose."

Proud moments occur for Anne and staff when they get positive feedback from members "...those who have just made some friends... those who have begun a significant relationship." It is "highly gratifying... to hear of engagements and marriages among members."

"Definitely we really enjoy running Science Connection... there are aggravations and anxieties, but it is a fun business."

Success is Service

Jane McLaughlin (l) and Gussie von Wellsheim (r)
Carpe Diem Coffee Roasting Company, Inc.
Main Street
North Berwick, ME 03906

Each week thousands of cups of Carpe Diem Coffee are consumed in New England. Carpe Diem Coffee Roasting Company uses nine different varieties from around the world to blend and flavor over 100 premium coffees. The partners, Jane and Gussie, roast, blend, flavor and package their coffee for restaurants, bakeries, specialty food shops, and for their burgeoning mail-order business.

Wanting a classic name, "Carpe Diem," meaning "seize the day," seemed a natural. It evokes a nice image... "Seize the day; start with a great cup of coffee." The physical demands, like handling 150 pound bags of raw coffee beans, pose no problems... "as owners you do what needs to be done."

Being long time Maine residents, with a real feel for "the taste of Maine," Gussie and Jane do not fear the proliferation of coffee roasters in this increasingly competitive business. After spending several months researching and writing a complete business plan, Jane and Gussie secured an SBA guaranteed loan from Key Bank of Maine in December of 1995. They use their business plan "almost constantly," reviewing it frequently and "taking advice from seasoned business people." With their emphasis on a "constantly superior product with consistently good service" they are confident that they are laying a good foundation for the long haul. Sales continue to grow steadily.

Jane and Gussie believe in giving back to the community. They are mentors themselves for aspiring women entrepreneurs, and they frequently donate their high quality product to local organizations and events.

They are proud of their business, and modestly "...want people to know us as 'that special little coffee company we discovered in Maine'."

A Strong Business Plan... And Success

Tracy Jobe
In Transit Personnel Inc.
207 - 2555
Eglinton Ave. E.
Scarborough, Ontario
M1K 5J1

Tracy Jobe supplies short and long-term replacement workers to the trucking and warehouse industries in Ontario. In May 1995, three months after opening, her company was making a profit.

Before starting her own business, Tracy spent several years as a dancer in musical theater. She then went back to university to study sociology. Finding few opportunities in social work, Tracy worked for her mother who owns a staffing industry company, but there were "personal issues, generational power struggles and I was looking for autonomy." As Tracy says, "I outgrew my role at her company and went into direct competition with her." Setting up a considerable distance from her mother, to minimize confrontation, Tracy has remained on good terms with her mother. Tracy found that "at first people did not take me seriously, but were curious to meet me." Tracy credits her success in the trucking business to an outgoing attitude, people skills, and knowledge about the trade from her mother.

Tracy is a strong believer in business plans. "I did a lot of research, then I went to the City of Scarborough's Small Business Help Centre. I was able to get financing from a bank, too, which is tough for small businesses, but I found the key is to build good relationships."

The offices open early and on-call service is available 24 hours a day. Service is the key. "We always follow up to see if a client was pleased with a driver and the work performed." A night dispatcher deals with the customers after hours but "since I take critical calls, I sleep with a pager by my bed."

After one year in business, Tracy grossed a remarkable $2.4 million in sales. She has already set up a profit-sharing plan and is planning more offices. "The business has taken more tenacity and commitment than I've ever had to give before. But returns have been far greater than sacrifices."

1998 Update: Expansion plans include Calgary and Vancouver, with an acquisition strategy for staffing companies limited by financing and management systems. Tracy has applied for Profit Magazine's *Fastest Growing Companies in Canada* Award for 1998/99. As Tracy says, "The road from small business owner to nation-wide coverage is a long and exciting one."

14

A Marketing Primer

Marketing is an enormous subject. It is possible here to touch only on a few fundamentals, while advising you to study what astute marketing observers are saying.

As important as anything in marketing is the development of a clear focus on your Market Target. With a precisely identified, measurable and understood Market Target, many of your other business variables fall into place. Then, associating your product/service with a simple, positive, message, repeated as many times and ways as you can, is the essence of marketing.

Market Target

> **Quick Marketing Tip**
>
> A "thank you" card is a most effective—and inexpensive—way to show a customer or client you appreciate their business. Get into the habit of using them by keeping a box handy… and sending them out immediately.

To market your company, you must answer two questions. Who are your target customers? How do you reach them?

Entrepreneurs often focus, mistakenly, more on the product or service than who is going to buy it, and how it is to be sold.

Defining your market target must be one of the first areas you study. Often one of the most difficult parts of outlining a specific market target is to narrow it down. If you are talking fast foods for instance, don't refer to the whole market and speak in billions of dollars. Rather, discuss the tiny segment of it at which you may be aiming. Then concentrate on describing just who are the customers for your niche, and how you'll reach those customers. Not only will you impress investors by describing realistic objectives, but you'll also help make your efforts more effective, because you won't be chasing the wrong market.

> *Weaving a net is better than paying for fish.*
>
> – Chinese Proverb

Once you have defined your target and how to reach it, stay focused when you get underway. This is tough because it's easy to try to appeal to everyone. It won't work. You'll be spread so thin, you won't be doing a good marketing job toward anyone.

In defining your market target, be aware of the enormous shifts from the traditional concept of broad target groups to the contemporary reality of narrower and narrower niche markets.

The consumer marketplace has become so differentiated, it is now discussed in terms of corners, of tiny slices of it. The challenge is to pick a niche from the great number out there—such as region, gender, socio-economic status, lifestyle, technological competence, very specific ethnic groups, generations, life stages, etc.

For example, Baby Boomers are often the only market force many marketers have identified and, of course they are a huge target. But, contrary to common expectation, they are not going to be like their parents.

Baby boomers were the youth market of 30 years ago and they intend to continue to be the youth market. They won't respond if talked to as older folk in a herd! You need to aim at small, precisely identified groups.

A principle to observe as you are developing communication and messages to your market target is to speak to them one-on-one, in a conversational style. Treat them as sensible people, sharing a conversation with you over coffee.

Primary Market Research Techniques

To define your market target, you will probably have to do some specific research. After you have gathered information from data bases, libraries, families, friends and experts, you probably still need to speak directly with your target public. (It is probably wise to talk to the trade too.)

Outlined on page 217 are research techniques you can apply yourself, or get applied for you at modest cost.

Advertising — Powerful and Persuasive

Advertising is another subject needing careful study for individual situations, and expertise from skillful practitioners. It requires assessment of variables such as the Market Target, copy, media, pricing, promotion, packaging, distribution and selling strategies.

Advertising needs to be persuasive. But above all, it must be credible to persuade, emotionally and logically. For help with your advertising, look through the Yellow Pages for advertising agencies. Agencies are chosen like any other service. Check out a number of them; study the work they do for others. Obtain references, and call them. While it is a plus to find an agency with experience in your field, it is much more important to find kindred people sympathetic to your goals and dreams.

As a new venture, your advertising budget is probably not going to be large. Yet it must work hard for you because you do not have any more to spend on advertising. Classic Catch 22!

You must grab your prospect's attention quickly and effectively. To do so, immediately offer the most alluring thing you can say about your product or service. If you can nab the prospect with those first few words, there is a chance that the rest of the ad will be noticed.

A difficult but effective way to develop headlines that will grab is to pretend they are for a billboard—And you have the motorist's attention for about three seconds. Thus, you have to distill your most powerful selling point down so it delivers its message in about two blinks of the eye!

One recognized technique for achieving this is to seek a "hot button." What hot button does your product or service "push" in your prospect... use it in the headline to grab your prospect's attention. Virtually every product or service sold has a hot button which can be associated with it. It is essential that **you** know the hot buttons that your products push. After all, who better than you should know. You and your staff will, or should, be pushing those hot buttons in all your sales activities, not just in advertising.

Learn to Love Networking

Networking is an essential business skill to master, to supplement what is often a small advertising and promotion budget. Fear of networking is a common problem... it can be intimidating walking into a roomful of strangers already enjoying themselves. Like so many other subjects touched upon in this book, a deliberate plan is suggested, designed to help you get business through consistent, organized networking.

- Do some research. Find out where and when groups that would attract your customers hold meetings.
- Set aside time to attend a few of these meetings. Make yourself attend!
- Remember that you may have only a few moments to make a good first impression. Consider your appearance very carefully. Dress to impress.
- Set a target number of people to meet.

> *Nobody can make you feel inferior without your consent.*
>
> – Eleanor Roosevelt

- Practice an introduction of yourself and your company—a short one!
- Be a great conversationalist—It's easy. Just ask questions of the other person. Ask questions, then ask some more. Then listen intently, to develop more good questions.
- When you arrive at any meeting, steel yourself and make the first introduction, perhaps to someone who is also alone. This becomes easy with practice, so practice everywhere.
- Exchange cards, telephone numbers, and do follow-up. Send a note and/or literature, ask for theirs. Send a clipping you think would interest them. If you promise to do something, do it, and as soon as possible. Stay in touch.
- Devise a system for remembering names and activities so that the next time you meet a person, you can greet them by mentioning both, e.g., "Hi Martha, how's the catering business?"

YES, Know What the Internet Can Do

If the Internet is old stuff to you, a review of basics never hurts anyone. This will be kept simple—to avoid quickly being out of date. So why, and how, should you access the Internet?

You need a computer, modem, printer and program software. Your best advisor is probably your "service provider," the service you select that actually connects you to the Internet. They often provide starter kits, pre-configured for their site, tested, proven to work and usually a free bonus for selecting them as your provider.

What will all this gear give you? Three things: communications, research and marketing.

Communication

The Internet is a communications medium, like a mailed letter. Electronic mail (or e-mail) is a speedy way to send messages through your computer, across town or the world. It is cheaper than long-distance telephone and more versatile. Anything you can put on your computer can be sent by e-mail. If you need to communicate by long-distance in this country or to other countries, your e-mail can probably pay for itself by the savings in long-distance costs alone.

Research

From your computer, you can obtain information on virtually any topic from anywhere in the world. You can have on-going contact with experts by simply subscribing to mailing lists and receiving information automatically and continuously on subjects which interest you.

Marketing

If a company is selling a product or service, if it values close relationships with good customers, if it conducts market research regularly, or if it has a big service or support department, marketing on the Internet can give a competitive advantage.

You will need to choose a service provider who sorts out Internet transmissions and allows you access to them for a price. There are many of these service providers to choose from. Again, use your advisors to help you define what you need from the Internet as a start towards selecting the service provider. Selection criteria are the same as for any other service—performance, professionalism and price.

Is the Internet for you?

The Internet is the information and communication phenomenon of our time, forecast to become the most powerful business medium the world has known. It is fun, too. But it may not be fun for you, or not useful for your business. That is fine, providing this is a carefully considered judgment reached by you and your advisors and not just the result of "techno-block." You just cannot afford not to know about the Internet and what it can do. You can be sure your competitors know!

Do You Want Your Own Site?

If some of your key customers, suppliers, and/or competitors are on-line, maybe you should be too! This however is no longer simply a matter of listing your name, address, products or services and then expecting to be bowled over by calls. Developing your own Site is a sophisticated job and it is important to seek expert, creative advice.

See page 176 for a list of Internet sites particularly useful for women at this time of writing. Be alert for new ones.

To Get, Try Giving

Marketing is getting noticed, being remembered. Sometimes it is also about helping others too. This is already clearly understood by entrepreneurial women—See many of the role-model women entrepreneur stories throughout this book.

As noted earlier, the National Foundation for Women Business Owners found that some 78% of women entrepreneurs participate in volunteer and charitable work, higher than "all business owners" at 56%, "all women" at 51% and "all adults" at 48%. Most of these entrepreneurs also encourage community participation by their employees.

Socially responsible marketing like this does not have to cost a fortune. For example, a nursery could plant flowers in inner city communities or give extra inventory to seniors' homes. Restaurants could deliver surplus food to shelters; specialty coffee shops could supply quality coffee to organizations and events; printing shops could donate photocopies, flyers, etc.

Benefits of giving are many. Employee morale is boosted, exposure for your company is increased, public awareness of social issues is increased. Although hard to quantify, you know that good work like this eventually boosts your profitability.

> *There are two ways of exercising strength—pushing down, and pulling up.*
>
> – Booker T. Washington

15

Trade Shows As Marketing Tools

One effective way to market is to participate in trade shows, a multi-billion-dollar a year industry. The US Trade Show Bureau found that it averages only one call to convert a trade show lead into a sale, compared to five cold calls. Deals are often made right at the show.

The Trade Show as a Marketplace

Research indicates that at a wholesale trade show, about one in five of the contacts will bring in quality sales or leads, with half of those leads resulting in orders within three months of the show.

Trade shows allow buyers to see competitors side by side and to comparison shop. This accelerates the process, permitting a sales team to do in a few days what might take several months in the field. Serious trade show prospects spend hours on site in a day. Get their attention with a well-planned exhibit and a pleasant, informed booth staff.

> **Don't Forget!**
>
> A survey revealed that the average trade show visitor spends about six hours studying exhibits and speaks to people at 17 booths. But only about 20% of trade show leads are later contacted by the exhibitor. 80% of the leads are ignored or forgotten!

Where to Start

If you think trade shows are marketing tools for you, start your research by calling colleagues and friendly competitors. Talk to your Chamber of Commerce about trade shows booked for your city a year in advance.

Check the record of the events you might consider. Most people will share experiences with you. How did the show work for them?

If the show you are considering is a repeat, get an information package from an earlier one. Look at the attendance figures, seminars and demonstrations offered, and the success of the show financially.

If you have never exhibited at any show, attend one or more as a visitor to get a feel for how they are run, and to judge how your product or service would measure up.

Points to Consider

- What kind of advertising and publicity campaign does the show follow? Is there a catalog published with names, addresses and description of each exhibitor's business?
- A successful show generally attracts previous participants back. Is there a different group of participants from one year to the next? If so, the trade show may not be working too well.
- Good attendance usually equals good sales. However, be cautious of events where exhibitors are only a part of a much larger promotion. Regardless of attendance figures, you don't want to be only a side show.
- While demonstrations are a proven aspect of trade shows, do not let them become entertainment which only attracts crowds and discourages serious buyers. Personal attention is still the path to success and you can rarely offer that while demonstrating.
- Scheduling demonstrations throughout the day will allow you to see what happens: check their effectiveness by tracking when big sales occur. Ask customers whether they saw your demonstration and if that helped them to make a decision to buy.
- Screening encourages a higher quality of participants in a show. For example, at many arts and craft shows, a jury selects participants. Another form of screening limits the number of exhibitors selling similar products or services.
- Traveling time to shows and money spent on expenses is justified if you call on other clients along the way.

Setting Goals and Objectives for Trade Show Marketing

Research indicates that nearly half the businesses in trade shows have no stated objectives for being there. If you have objectives for specific shows, contact the manager and ask for a planning guide and prices on various items. Draft a plan relating to your business.

Set goals high, but not out of sight. The primary purpose of being there is to sell. **Trade shows are an expensive form of advertising, but an inexpensive way of selling.** They are also an opportunity to do a survey of your market. Take advantage of the concentration of visitors; gauge reactions to your product line or service and your prices.

Some suggested goals:

- Sell a certain volume at the show.
- Make contacts for follow-up sales.
- Introduce a new product or service and assess its acceptance.
- Demonstrate products or techniques you could not normally take to a customer.
- Develop market areas outside your normal territory.
- Line up distributors, dealers or sales representatives.
- Introduce a new image.
- Network with competitors and other exhibitors; pick up ideas, and compare notes on suppliers, other shows and fairs; develop new outlets for your goods.

Planning

Don't plan in a vacuum! Contact the exhibit management and discuss your proposals before you commit. Don't think in terms of being able to correct mistakes, call for extra help or dash back to the shop for more props just because you are in easy commuting distance. Plan as though you lived 100 miles away!

See page 219 for specific questions about planning for trade shows.

Creating an Image

Everything you do, say and display should be consistent with the image you wish to project, both in the show and at other times. This is an important decision, to which you should give considerable thought, quite separately from shows. It's part of your overall marketing strategy.

Exhibitor's Kit

An exhibitor's kit obtained from the show's management provides information on show rules and on-site services. Read it to avoid surprises! There may be restrictions on what you can use or do in the booth. If there are exhibitor meetings in advance, try to attend and ask questions.

Here are some of the most likely optional services you will encounter:

- Booth cleaning, carpeting, and extra security
- Plants, photography, custom signage, and furniture not included in the basic rental
- Audio/visual equipment, telephone service
- Extra electrical service

The Budget Process

Budgeting will play a key role in the success of your trade show. You must have an idea what a given trade show will cost you. Bear in mind though that whether you are developing a total booth design, basic signage, graphics or some small display units, you will be able to use them again.

Booth development is your major expense. You might rent a booth through the trade show organization, and save headaches over installation, transportation or removal.

Use your Exhibitor's Kit, do research, and come up with a budget. Do a table listing estimated costs, including insurance. The show management usually provides a basic on-site insurance package, but you may need additional coverage during traveling as well as at the show. After the show, complete the table with actual costs. Noting actual versus estimated expenses will be helpful for planning your next event.

See page 220 for budget items you need to consider.

16

Tips For Survival — and Growth

Prevention is Best

Each year, many entrepreneurs run into difficulties and declare bankruptcy. Dreams are shattered, resources are squandered and staff lose employment. The cost to the economy is enormous.

Although failure may not always be avoidable, it is far from inevitable. Studies of small business insolvency invariably reach the same conclusion: most small business failures result from poor management by the owner. Business survival doesn't happen by formula, nor by accident. By continuously monitoring your business closely, you develop a keen sense of your strengths and weaknesses, and can adjust before alarm bells ring. This chapter provides tips for coping and surviving.

Watch for Warning Signs

Watch for signs that the economy of your community may be changing. Such as:

- Declines in purchases of new appliances and equipment because people defer purchases or save money by repairing existing items.
- Loan applications being turned down by lenders, especially for long-established firms. Talk to credit officers.
- Retailers offering drastic special offers.
- Suppliers being quicker to demand payment and less willing to extend credit.
- Personal monies being used to pay business expenses.
- Increased talk about mergers, acquisitions, take-overs and bailouts.

> *I am hurt but I am not slain. I'll lay me down and bleed a while.*
> *And then I'll rise and fight again.*
>
> – Sir Andrew Barton

Chat with Key People in the Community

Not all news makes the local papers. So talk regularly with people who move around the community, such as:

- Bank officers and managers; inquire about local trends.
- Police officers, bailiffs and sheriffs. Ask about the frequency of break-ins, hold-ups or fraud.
- Owners of general stores, hardware stores. They often know who is suffering economically.
- Auctioneers and Realtors. Are foreclosures and sales of household effects increasing?

Be Suspicious of Other People's Swift Growth

Rapid success can be deadly. Demands of expansion can drain time and financial resources as well as customers and suppliers. Some possible clues are:

- Employees who seem rushed off their feet.
- Frequent line-ups of customers.
- Shipments being delayed or incomplete.

Detect Other People's Financial Mismanagement

Entrepreneurs have temperaments best suited to promoting ideas and sales. Too often, books drift into disrepair and the business suffers. Hints can be:

- Invoices take weeks to arrive.
- Billing errors go unnoticed or uncorrected by them.
- Vague answers when you ask how well their business is doing.

Spot Signs of Other People's Inadequate Planning

Learn to notice the symptoms of companies out of touch with the marketplace due to negligence or ignorance. Some clues:

- Inconsistent unit pricing or inconsistent shipping costs.
- Frequent price changes.

Note Poor Employer/Employee Relationships

- High degree of absenteeism, turnover.
- Surly, unenthusiastic and unhelpful staff.
- Persistent early closing.

Notice Other People's Problems with Stress and Time

Running a small business is never easy. If the day-to-day difficulties become too overwhelming, the toll on the owner's health can become apparent. Telltale hints:

- Repeated lateness for meetings.
- Appointments frequently broken or rescheduled.
- Haggard or unkempt personal appearance.

Monitor Your Business Health

Financial illness rarely occurs overnight. Signs of danger are visible much earlier. Watch for typical symptoms; work to prevent the trouble from becoming life-threatening.

- **Avoid "Shoebox" Accounting**

  You won't thrive unless timely financial information is available. Assess your accounting:
  - How adequate is your record-keeping?
  - Are your financial statements prepared frequently enough?
  - Do you know your cost of goods and profit margin for each product?
  - Are accounts payable and accounts receivable listings aged?
- **Prepare Forecasts Regularly**
  - Do you prepare monthly forecasts for your business, comparing actual performance to forecasts; making adjustments for new conditions?
  - Do you compare a cash flow budget with the actual cash flow?
- **Preserve Your Cash Flow**

  Often businesses fail because they use their operating line to pay for capital equipment, turning the problem into one of cash flow. Then they go to the bank and are denied a capital loan. Meanwhile, now short of cash, suppliers are knocking on their doors and staff have to be paid.

  The cash flowing in and out of your business can be misleading. To maintain a healthy cash flow, you obviously need to generate more revenue than expenses—But you need to generate the revenue in advance. Otherwise, you won't be able to meet expenses as they arrive. The trick is to regulate this flow carefully.

  Owners often focus too much on bringing money in and ignoring how much money is leaving. Suddenly they find themselves short of cash and go bankrupt, even though they are showing an overall profit. Even a fairly small cash deficit can be enough to force you out of business if you can't make a payroll or clear debts with suppliers.

- **Avoid Huge Cash Outlays**
  Buying something outright is not always prudent. Leasing is one way to conserve cash or capital.
  - Always know your cash position.
  - Consider leasing anything which depreciates—such as computers, cars and telephone systems.
  - Ask to purchase equipment and supplies via monthly installments.
- **Set Payment Goals**
  Regulate outgoing cash; ensure that your current account isn't drained.
  - Stagger payments of accounts payable throughout the month.
  - Suppliers should receive cheques no more than a day or two earlier than their due date. If no date is specified, assume you have 30 days.
  - Take advantage of early payment discounts.
- **Use Credit Card Companies**
  For retailers, credit cards are often the next best thing to cash. Cash is returned promptly without you needing to chase payment.
  - But check out the transaction fees: the charge is minimal if you join an organization such as retail merchants' associations, manufacturers' associations, a hotel association or the Better Business Bureau.
  - Look for the lowest rate available and don't be afraid to negotiate.
  - Reduce your paper work by only accepting one card if your credit card sales volumes aren't high.
- **Obtain Credit References**
  Many businesses must extend credit to remain competitive and to increase sales, but thorough credit checks on all new customers will decrease the odds of unpaid bills.
  - Ask for the name of the customer's bank, at least two references, and verify them all.
  - If your customer is a business, ask for the names of three of their suppliers. Then call these people and ask about their experience with your new customer.
  - Have a three order trial period; these orders are paid COD.
  - Contact the Better Business Bureau and find out if your new customer has a solid business past.
  - If you suspect a deal is too good to be true, it probably is. Redouble your efforts to check it out.
- **Monitor Individual Customer Accounts Carefully and Regularly**
  Even after good references, scrutinize customer accounts regularly.
  - If you notice changes in payment pattern, update credit checks. Phone other suppliers and find out if they too are experiencing problems with this company.

- If you have a delinquent account, stop extending credit immediately and switch to a cash-only basis.

- **Don't Get Squeezed for Cash**
  You are the owner. Don't trust the responsibility of monitoring your cash flow to someone else simply because you find the task unpleasant.

Recover Receivables

Having overdue accounts receivable is a serious and typical cause of weak cash flow. Some sensible ways to speed up collection and improving your cash flow position are:

- **Always Invoice Early**
  Send out your invoices within 24 hours of delivery. The sooner your customer has your bill, the sooner you will be paid.
- **Make Paying Easy for Customers**
  Take a little time to ensure your customers can pay you easily without snags. For new customers, call before you bill to find out the correct individual and address, and invoice directly to that person's attention.
- **Ask for a Deposit**
  If you are custom-designing a product for a client or preparing samples of custom-designed products, ask for a partial payment in advance. Then, plan so you get paid as work is completed.
- **Set Payment Terms**
  State prominently on the invoice what payment terms are. Establish whether the payment date is from the date of invoice, the date goods were received, or the statement date.
- **Avoid Discounts and Penalties**
  Discounts for early payment or penalties for overdue accounts are not worth the effort. Customers often take the discount and yet still pay late.
- **Act Swiftly on Overdues**
  The squeaky wheel gets paid—The silent one doesn't. Chances of collecting debts diminish rapidly after 90 days. Don't assume the cheque is in the mail, phone long before 90 days are up.

Collect Overdues

- **Age receivables each month.** Place unpaid bills in a special file.
- **Plan collection strategy.** Collecting is a process; phone calls, notes, letters and negotiations. You work to recover the money and keep your customer's goodwill.
- **Phone.** Cheaper than a letter and much more effective. Phone the day before the invoice is due to remind about payment. Offer to pick up the payment personally.
- **Be courteous, but persistent.** Always assume the other party can and will pay, given enough prodding. Don't become angry.
- **Keep records** of every phone call and letter sent.
- **Send a reminder letter** after 30 days, or a statement with an "overdue" sticker.
- **Send a follow-up** letter a week later.
- **Be flexible and willing to negotiate.** If the account is really old, recognize that any payment is better than none.
- **Apply to a collection agency**, as a last resort.
- **Alternatively**, use a friend to handle collections. Offer a percentage—This may cost less than a collection agency.

Stay Afloat

- **Demonstrate Good Faith.** At 60 days, start paying vendors any way you can. Call first. If you can't pay all the bills, try to negotiate a partial payment or extended terms without penalty.
- **Protect Your Credit Rating.** Keep making payments, even if small. If suppliers decide to deal with you only for cash, it could be disastrous.
- **Negotiate Terms Firmly.** In an economic downturn, you have leverage to negotiate terms from major suppliers; everybody is experiencing loss of business. Haggle for the best terms you can get.
- **Establish Payment Priorities.** Don't focus on those who shout loudest. First to be paid includes the tax-man, major suppliers and bankers. These people have the power to shut you down!
- **Review Records Regularly.** Check accounts payable records frequently. Know your situation.
- **Consider Factoring.** Factoring is the selling of a company's accounts receivable for cash. This produces cash quickly, though you are still responsible for bad debts.
- **Make Deposits Daily.** Feed your bank account each day.

Reduce Costs

Controlling expenses is easier than generating income or penetrating new markets. You don't have to influence someone else to spend money. You simply have to persuade yourself to stop spending it.

When cash is short, a business should always look inward to reduce expenses before looking outward to increase sales or raise new financing. Scrutinize every fixed and variable expense incurred over the past quarter and then compare these actual costs with those projected in your last forecast.

- **Buy Used Rather Than New**
  Money can be saved by buying used office and other equipment from auctions and government surplus sales.
- **Join Discount Warehouses**
  Discount houses offer considerable savings without requiring membership fees. Credit cards and commercial accounts are often accepted.
- **Bargain with Suppliers**
  Negotiate for the best price with wholesalers and suppliers. Remember they could be hurting too if money is tight. They may offer considerable discounts on larger than normal shipments. Offer to pay cash immediately, if you can, to help their cash flow in return for further savings. Check out other suppliers too. They may offer sizable "introductory" reductions to secure a new customer.
- **Drop Unprofitable Lines**
  Take each product line or type of service you provide and analyze its costs. Examine whether it is absorbing its share of overhead; if not, consider discontinuing this item.
- **Save on Advertising**
  Since advertising and promotion are a critical link to your customers, try to avoid cutting these activities. Instead, look for ways to generate free publicity for your business:
  - Hold promotional events. Invite the media.
  - Write a press release about something new in your business—such as introducing an innovative product line or securing a large contract. Submit it with a small ad to local newspapers.
  - Offer to do free interviews on radio and TV shows.
  - Listen to hot line shows and then phone in your opinion. Include some reference to your business and its name.
  - Offer to give free talks and presentations to local community groups.
- **Reduce Overhead by Cutting Key Variable Costs**
  Monitor office and warehouse temperatures.
  - Turn off lights and equipment at the end of the day.

- Replace ordinary light bulbs with more efficient ones using less power.
- Spend less time on long distance calls by making use of form letters.
- Send fax messages after 6:00 p.m. or before 8:00 a.m. when phone rates are cheaper.
- Use pagers rather than cellular phones.
- If your business uses much long-distance, consider e-mail.

♦ **Retreat to the Home**
Consider operating from home. A spare bedroom becomes an office; a basement or garage acts as a studio or warehouse. Overheads are shared with your domestic expenses; computer and telephone technology can keep you in touch with customers without a loss in professional image.

♦ **Share Space and Services**
If your home isn't suitable, consider reducing space and staff and overhead costs by using packaged office services, or renting space with congenial associates. Many centers have office space and boardrooms available for rent, some even on a daily basis.

♦ **Review Service Contracts**
Conserve cash by obtaining at least three bids for work contracted out and for service arrangements such as janitorial cleaning or maintenance and repairs. Consider reducing your insurance coverage or increasing the deductible. The threat of cancellation may help negotiate a reduction in carrying charges from your lender.

♦ **Maximize Use of Staff**
Trimming staff is cost effective only if remaining employees can operate the business. Often the way to reduce labor costs is to adjust levels rather than numbers of employees:

- Redistribute staff, including clerical staff, so they are on the shop floor when most customer support is needed.
- If demand for personnel fluctuates, use temporaries and part-time assistance, whenever possible.
- When work is slow, have employees perform other work such as janitorial duties or warehouse maintenance rather than sit idle, or worse yet, being laid off.

♦ **Barter and Exchange Services**
When you barter, you trade the cost of your product or service—plus your profit—with another business. This helps you increase purchasing power while retaining cash. But keep in mind that bartering is as taxable as other transactions. Consult IRS officials regarding tax implications.

♦ **Lease Capital Equipment**
Leasing is a way of acquiring vehicles, or plant equipment without depleting your cash reserves. However, leasing can be complicated. Discuss it with your accountant.

Control Inventory

Companies often make the mistake of tying up too much cash in inventories. Look for ways to prevent inventories from building up. In the process liquidate inventory for always needed cash.

- **Monitor Flow of Merchandise Weekly**
  Move to a perpetual inventory tracking system which provides current data about individual product lines. Count inventory once and then subtract each item as it is sold, producing weekly tallies. Add purchase totals as new stock arrives. This system gives you an immediate inventory count and helps you to assess which items are moving.
- **Focus on Bestsellers**
  Review your sales carefully. Concentrate on moving high volumes of what you are selling well. When times are lean, this is the best strategy for staying afloat. Limit reordering to these fast-movers so the same cash is being swiftly recycled.
- **Sell Slow-Movers Quickly**
  Liquidate as much obsolete stock as possible with promotions. Remember, a dollar in the hand is worth ten on the shelf.
- **Produce Small-Ticket Items**
  When the economy is uncertain, customers reduce spending, especially on big-ticket items. Increase your turnover: offer smaller scale purchases.
- **Look for Local Suppliers**
  Inventory levels can be trimmed if you can locate suppliers near you.
- **Analyze Supplier Discounts**
  Suppliers will offer incentives to induce you to purchase more than you need. Be cautious. Compare the value of the discount against the cost of tying up your cash.
- **Keep Inventory Low**
  Avoid producing too much stock in anticipation of sales or ordering too many raw materials. The aim should be to ship orders on time easily without stock-piling.
- **Streamline by Using a Computer**
  Consider installing a computerized inventory control system that continually updates records on a product-by-product basis. The cost can easily pay for itself in savings. Check computer magazines for addresses of "shareware" suppliers, programs offered on a free-trial basis.

Improve Your Rating

- Be well dressed—Most people respect conservative attire.
- Invest in good quality accessories—pen, watch, briefcase, etc.
- Never knock the competition.
- Be on time and deliver everything you promise.
- Never argue with customers—not always right, they are always customers.
- Look for opportunities to do something extra.
- Plan and prepare each appointment in advance.
- Write thank you notes to each new customer or prospect.

Attract New Sales

Good marketing begins and ends with the customers... you must understand and be current about your market.

Before searching for new clients and customers, try stimulating more business with current ones. Persuading new customers to make a purchase takes more effort than persuading past customers. Go for warm calls before making cold calls.

- **Pamper Regulars**
  Honor regular, profitable, and loyal customers—people you cannot afford to lose.
  - Offer preferential treatment such as sneak previews or customer appreciation events, discounts off new work or increased orders.
  - Make your best customers feel honored by sending a small gift (perhaps barter for this with a supplier) or a special thank-you card. Follow up with a phone call a few days later. Be discreet though. Don't let this look cheap!
- **Reactivate Old Accounts**
  Wade through old client lists, order books and sales ledgers. Find people who haven't been customers for a while. Let them know you are still in business. Try to discern why they left you. Demonstrate strong interest in their current needs.
- **Increase Each Sale with Add-Ons.**
  Aim to enlarge each sale by encouraging customers to purchase more:
  - When customers place orders, suggest that you can give them a much better deal if they would buy three units rather than one.
  - Offer low-cost accessories. Package your items so that small extras can be offered, such as cleaning kits, attachments or spare parts.

- **Provide Incentives**
  - Offer multiple purchase schemes: a customer making a certain number of purchases gets the next one free.
  - Offer gifts as incentives for customer recommendations and word-of-mouth referrals.
  - Offer discounts for special-interest groups, especially students, seniors or non-profit societies, all of whom can be very price conscious.

> **Quick Tip**
>
> Use existing customers to unlock a new direction for your business. Don't ask them what they want— They'll probably give pat answers like something cheaper, faster, better, etc. Instead, ask them what they need. Find out what they presently can't obtain at all.

- **Offer Necessities**
  Expand your range of products or services to include ones which will keep customers coming back for more. For example, a kitchen store should promote low-price pots and pans for which demand is constant rather than non-essential appliances such as electric knife sharpeners.
- **Look for Clones of Best Customers**
  Construct a profile of regular customers you presently have: size, location, type of operation, level of business, etc. Then hunt for similar firms to target for new sales. Clones of your best customers are your best bet for boosting sales.
- **Diversify Your Range of Clients**
  Try broadening your customer base. For example, try cross-selling with a partner. Find someone already selling in a new market and offer assistance with selling each other's goods. Try inserting promotional material in with your partner's and pay for a joint mailing. Share marketing costs, piggy-back on each other's sales contacts and seek cost-effective ways to break into a new market.
- **Offer Something Unusual**
  The more you can look different, the more people will see a reason to choose you. Search for ways to add value to products and services without increasing costs directly:
  - Use brighter or sturdier packaging for products. Offer to gift wrap.
  - Where possible, supply door-to-door delivery on phoned in orders to assist disabled customers or those unable to leave home.
  - Provide special on-site installation and advice follow-up. This is particularly useful with high-tech equipment such as computers.
- **Get the Product into People's Hands**
  - Hold demonstrations for target client groups.
  - At social events, such as bingos, offer products as prizes.

- Offer customers free home trials, money-back guarantees and other incentives for testing the product.
- Hold complimentary seminars or night school workshops that make use of your product or which advertise your expertise.

Analyze Competitors

Sometimes survival is threatened by new competitors. Respond by analyzing their operations thoroughly. For instance, when GM realized the Japanese auto companies were beating them, in the mid 80's, they had their engineers strip down the import cars to see what the Japanese were doing differently.

- **Speak to Your Competitors' Customers, and Your Lost Customers**
  Stand outside their stores and ask people as they leave why they shop there. Ask questions like, "What do you like about this company?" "How long have you been coming here?" and "What would make you switch to another store?" Phone up customers who you know have switched from you. Ask them courteously what caused them to switch.
- **Assess the Financial Status of Competitors**
  For public companies, request annual reports. For private companies, piece together whatever data you can obtain by asking previous employees, suppliers, searching through local trade directories, and checking out databases at local Chambers of Commerce. Can you see where competitors are saving costs? Can you tell where their market share is? Can you anticipate where they will invest or expand?
- **Study Your Competitor's Product Line or Services**
  Look through their catalogs and price lists. Walk around their stores. Where do holes exist which you could fill? How do prices compare with yours? Are their materials better? Is their service better?
- **Look at Competitor's Advertising and Publicity Material**
  Get on their mailing lists. Read their brochures. Discover what marketing strategies are being used. Can you spot their weaknesses?
- **Purchase a Product or Service From Your Competitor**
  How does it feel to be a customer? Is the quality of service better than yours? Can you see areas for improvement? Can you see mistakes your company is making?
- **Look for Competitors Going Out of Business**
  During hard times, some competitors may be forced into bankruptcy. This offers you an opportunity to make offers for their stock and supplies, purchase mailing and customer lists.

Uncover Problems

Besides looking at ways to increase sales, also consider why current sales may be stagnating and what to do about it:

- **Discover your Level of Customer Satisfaction**
  Quiz current customers. Mail them a questionnaire with invoices or phone them up. Ask customers why they use you, how they found you, how they rate your products. Ask what they like and don't like about doing business with you.
- **Perform a Service Audit**
  Contact customers and ask what is important to them about their contact with you: on the phone, on your premises, via invoice and statements, etc. How do they feel treated when they make a complaint? Do they refer you to others? Guard against the I-see-them-every-day-so-I-know-what-they-think attitude. Discover if the needs of customers are changing.

Cope with the Pressure

You can't succeed in business if you don't have fundamentally good work habits. A lot of succeeding is just staying at your desk through sheer willpower and doing what needs to be done.

When sales are low and profits are slim, your anxiety level is raised. Since you function less efficiently under stress, mistakes or errors occur. Break out of this vicious cycle by getting control of your time:

- **Keep to a Regular Work Schedule**
  Don't let crisis management become a habit. Stick as much as possible to regular working hours. A consistent timetable helps keep you on track. Try to schedule each daily activity, remembering to leave sufficient time and some flexibility for when things occur beyond your control. Force yourself to go home, shut out problems, relax with friends and family, talk about something other than business.
- **Change Attitude About Time**
  If you work all day and feel little is achieved, try keeping a record of how you spent each hour of the day. Any time spent doing one thing is time no longer available for doing something else. Time is finite—Budget it.
- **Use Rituals for Starters**
  Some days, getting started isn't easy. So begin the day with something pleasurable. If you like chatting on the phone, start your day by phoning customers and prospects. Whatever your pleasure, make this into a ritual.

- **Prioritize Tasks**
  Write down priorities for business in terms of high, medium and low tasks. Be flexible. Priorities often change. Make sure staff know if you change your mind. Use in-baskets, self-adhesive notes, flipcharts and wall boards to communicate priorities to everyone.
- **Make Daily Lists, Improve Your Organization**
  Make a list of things to be done and cross off the tasks as you complete them. This will give you a psychological lift and help the stress of trying not to forget everything you have to do—and the panic of remembering something missed. Arrange your filing system and workspace so the most frequently used items are the ones within reach.
- **Invent Daily Deadlines**
  Setting times and dates to complete a project will help keep you focused. You'll be surprised how many things get done. Break large tasks into small ones and give them separate deadlines. Reward yourself as you meet each deadline, by doing something that gives you a lift.
- **Deal with Timewasters**
  Avoid wasting time on clients who are just seeking free information or customers who probably won't place an order. Assume the best but look for clues to help you "qualify" the other person:
  - Ask specific questions about the customer's buying interests.
  - Ask for the customer/client's name. Serious shoppers will identify themselves while others will be more reluctant.
- **Delegate Tasks**
  Entrepreneurs and owner/managers find handing over responsibility to staff members difficult. Properly train someone now to take over your less important duties, so your time is freed up for more important managerial tasks. Don't waste time in supervision. Your employees need to make decisions themselves to build morale and competence. Remember, there is a difference between delegation and assignment. You delegate a task when you give the employee power to make judgments. You assign a task when you show a staff member how to do something and coach them throughout. You shouldn't delegate a task before having assigned it.
- **Be More Decisive**
  When facing difficulties, stop for a moment to determine how serious the problem is. It's better to cancel an ailing project and complete others well, rather than struggling to finish all of them badly.
- **Use Mottoes and Maxims**
  Keep your spirits up with the reinforcement that famous sayings can provide. Use inspirational quotations above your desk or on the office door—and in staff rooms.

- **Turn Negatives into Positives**
  When things aren't going well, persuade yourself to be optimistic. Practice positive self-talk, give yourself compliments, reflect on previous accomplishments. Treat failure as something temporary. Regard mistakes as learning experiences. Avoid being in the company of the cynical or critical. Keep your sense of humor. Your positive approach will influence associates and employees.

Reconsider Your Staffing

Managing personnel effectively can be your greatest asset or worst failure. It's worth time and effort to recruit and keep the best employees. Make continuing efforts to upgrade their skills. Good employees will be appreciative of your interest in them.

Demonstrate sensitivity to staff needs. Show you appreciate a problem; commit to correcting it as soon as possible.

- **Share the Work Around**
  Instead of laying off employees, consider work sharing, especially when slowdowns may be short-lived. Reduce shifts by an hour or so for everyone. Put everyone on a four-day week and stagger the use of staff.
- **Encourage staff participation**
  Increase productivity through employee involvement. You may be surprised by what others have to offer.
  - Share your management problems and seek advice. Hold lunchroom discussions of problems where solutions are brainstormed.
  - Place a suggestion box next to the coffee machine and ask for ideas for improving methods and profitability.
  - Pool resources and talent. Set up work teams of three or four people. Ask them to be accountable for tasks like "removing" a production line problem or "solving" a record-keeping problem or "improving" an inefficient order-processing system.

> *The question is not how to get everything I want—*
> *but do I want everything I have!*
>
> – Unknown

- **Recognize Staff Effort and Success**
  Show appreciation for extra contributions staff make to the business, especially in troubled times. Small, frequent recognition works best.
  - Be generous with your thanks. Acknowledge people personally and in company newsletters or staff news.
  - Instead of monetary rewards, provide tokens of appreciation such as gifts, cards, or extra days off.
- **Promote Staff Without Additional Salary**
  Even during lean times, try to promote staff who show leadership and ambition. If staff feel you wish them to succeed, they are more likely to remain with you.
  - Try giving staff a more imposing title for their existing job. Change "secretary" to "office manager." Turn "warehouse supervisor" into "warehouse manager"
  - Delegate some of your administrative duties to an assistant who becomes "acting manager." Often the pride of wearing a new hat will compensate for extra workload.
  - Reward performance with perks like use of company vehicles on weekends or extra discounts on merchandise, etc.
- **Reduce Staffing Costs**
  Sometimes you can beat the high cost of maintaining employees—or hiring new ones—by using volunteers.
  - Phone local schools and colleges and offer to provide work experience for students for a few hours each week. Many private business colleges need practicums for students.
  - Write to universities and colleges, requesting students to do projects for you.
  - Put small ads in local newspapers, at community centers, etc. asking for part-time volunteer assistance.
  - Take advantage of employment incentives offered by local governments which may provide a portion of a new employee's wage in return for on-the-job training. Use government sponsored "hire-a-student" services.
- **Use Family Members and Friends**
  Pressing relatives or friends into service can be a sensible way to obtain extra hands. But be sure to record their help so that when your business improves, you can repay them.
  - Have teenagers run errands. Ask the family to assist with typing and filing on weekends.
  - Have friends drive you to airports or bus stations. Use neighbors for emergency child care or to receive parcels.

Improve What You Have to Offer

Modifying what you already do may be easier than coming up with new ideas. So, while alert for new opportunities, also look for ways to make simple adjustments to current offerings. Brainstorm. How could you:

- **Manufacture an item more cheaply?**
- **Improve a sales presentation?**
- **Improve the value of the item?**
- **Make basic improvements in products or services?**
- **Take advantage of trends.**
- **Sell Information, Expertise**
  Information is now a commodity. Ever-widening use of the personal computer permits better storage and faster transmission. So look for ways you can sell information and expertise:
  - Produce guidebooks.
  - Sell or rent contact lists.
  - Offer expertise in workshops and night school classes.
  - Provide after-sales consulting or pre-sales advice.
- **Offer a Relaxed Atmosphere**
  Look for ways to brighten workspace for employees and customers:
  - Use paintings and wall decorations to brighten rooms.
  - Use creative designs in packaging and promotion.
  - Offer special services for clients such as free parking and free coffee.
  - Use music, good lighting and plants.
- **Offer Quality Not Quantity**
  The desire for individual expression is replacing conformity. Give your attention to short-run production of high quality products.
  - Produce customized and one-of-a-kind items.
  - Tailor items for specific niche markets.
  - Tighten your quality control and strive for zero defects.
  - Offer specialized service for customers willing to pay extra.
  - Produce first-class work and guarantee it.
- **Appeal to the Senior Consumer**
  The graying of the population is underway. Look for ways to attract a senior audience:
  - Make products lighter and easier to hold.
  - Consider providing medicinal and hygiene items or handyman support and safety devices.
  - Link your products to the lifestyle of seniors, e.g., travel packages.

- **Go Environmental Green**
  We are finally concerned with the environment. Tailor your business to an increasingly environmentally-conscious public:
  - Advertise that you provide environmentally-friendly products and that you recycle.
  - Design and package your products so they are safer on the environment. Make better use of recycled raw materials.
  - Be sure you live up to your promises and claims!

Look for openings

- **Study Corporate News**
  Keep an eye out for firms going bankrupt. Move in to fill the gap. If a business fails, demand won't have evaporated; another supplier or outlet will usually be needed. Offer to purchase customer lists, existing stock, fixtures and accounts receivable of companies going into receivership.
- **Use Repairs as Sales**
  In hard times, people are motivated to salvage life out of old equipment rather than buy a replacement. So, generate income by offering to service old equipment, even on items sold by competitors.
- **Don't Get Depressed — Get Active.**
  People are always an excellent source of ideas and leads.
  - Talk to everyone you meet about your business. Chat to people in supermarkets or bank line-ups. Treat strangers as potential customers. Raise your profile—Mention what you sell to each person you meet.
  - Join local groups such as the Chamber of Commerce; attend business seminars in your area.
  - Make friends with librarians and pick their brains for information.

Negotiate New Financing

Failure is only an opportunity to begin again, more intelligently.

If, despite your best efforts, you begin to see the threat of bankruptcy looming, don't wait until the last moment to obtain additional funds or explore re-financing options. Only loan sharks lend money in a hurry.

- **Keep your Bank Informed**
  Establish a good banking relationship in advance. Bankers and other lenders are unlikely to advance funds to people in dire straits if they don't already know them well.
  - Always try to arrange lines of credit and overdraft protection in advance when your cash flow is healthy—just in case you run into difficulty—rather than applying later when you actually need the cash.

- If you think you are headed for a cash flow problem, phone to let your banker know well ahead of time. Seek to negotiate agreed strategies for handling the problem. Ask for overdraft protection and seek extensions on the due dates for loan payments.

♦ **Have Explanations and Plans Ready**
Prepare your case before asking for additional funds. Demonstrate awareness and responsibility for your financial difficulties by describing how you ran into trouble and how profits can be re-generated. Prepare a written proposal. Bring along financial statements and evidence in trade publications, showing optimism for your line of business.

♦ **Seek Creative Alternatives**
Finding additional funds is never easy.
- Search for motivated bankers. Phone and ask for the senior lending Officer. Check whether loans in your industry would be considered.
- Offer non-capital security such as patents and copyrights.
- Consider asking your suppliers or employees for financial assistance, people who have a vested interest in your success. Ask if they would be willing to help you.
- Place a small ad in the business section of national newspapers or trade journals to attract investors and be willing to pay a private investor a higher rate of return than they can achieve elsewhere.
- If you have an insurance policy with a cash value, you may be able to borrow against it. Interest rates can be low, allowing you to pay off other loans at higher rates.
- Speak to lawyers, accountants and business professionals. They often encounter clients who may be willing to invest or help refinance your company's operations. A referral fee may be charged.

♦ **Shop Around For Best Deals**
Lending money can be a very competitive business.
- Watch for new financial institutions or branches opening locally. These will be keen to attract new customers.
- Ask friends and business associates where they do their banking. Compare rates and experiences. If you consider switching banks, mention recommendations and bring written introductions.

♦ **Seek Help As Well As Cash**
Refinancing is often easier to obtain if you make lenders feel involved and listen to their advice. Benefit from their knowledge and experience.
- Ask about ways of consolidating your existing debts into a single loan to reduce interest payments.
- Ask about restructuring your debt.

- **Secure Standby Financing**
  If you doubt the level of commitment shown by present lenders, you may need to seek standby financing. Remember, the fees can be costly.
  - Approach venture capitalists, investment syndicates and other non-institutional bodies. These investors can arrange guaranteed funds or bridging loans in the event of emergencies such as a called-in loan or an exhausted line of credit. Be warned: you may have to offer some equity or shared ownership.
  - Apply for additional credit cards. In an emergency, the lines of immediate credit and cash offered by credit card companies—typically at $5,000 or more per card—have saved many businesses. But use with caution and only as a last resort… they are very expensive.

Network

> **Karma Repair Kit: Items 1-4***
>
> 1. Get enough food to eat,
>   and eat it.
> 2. Find a place to sleep
>   where it is quiet,
>   and sleep there.
> 3. Reduce intellectual and
>   emotional noise until you reach
>   the silence of yourself,
>   and listen to it.
> 4.

Women entrepreneurs sometimes feel overwhelmed, balancing the demands of work, family and community. They try to combine the duties of parent, employer and citizen; raising loving, non-violent children, providing empathetic direction to employees, and being active in community affairs.

It is important to remember there are other women doing exactly this, and connecting with them is vital; supporting and working together is important for common goals, whether organizing carpools and child care, a potluck dinner or neighborhood improvements.

We all wish to live healthy, balanced lives. This includes some combination of four elements, governed by individual and personal priorities:

1. family and friends (loving, supportive relationships)
2. spirituality (a belief system providing inner strength and direction)
3. hobbies (recreation, time for relaxation and play)
4. work (a career, profession, sense of productivity)

---

* From *The Pill versus The Springhill Mine Disaster*, Richard Brantigan, Dell, 1968, p.8. [Yes, this is an accurate quote.]

17

Role Model Women Entrepreneurs

A Caring Business

Evelyn Valcourt
Evelyn's Wig &
Breast Prosthetic Service
Box 37
Lorette, Manitoba
R0A 0Y0

After managing wig stores, Evelyn decided to build a cranial and breast prosthesis business in her rural home, 15 minutes east of Winnipeg. Here she provides a setting of calm confidentiality for dealing with the traumas of hair loss or mastectomy; even a quiet room for those needing a few moments to themselves.

Booking only three appointments daily, Evelyn gives individualized, compassionate care, restoring self-esteem, confidence and personal dignity. "There can be no hurrying with the work I do… it may take me all morning to be certain of a customer's needs."

Evelyn inventories over 300 headwear, related hair care products and breast prosthetic devices. Clients, quickly becoming friends, range from very young to seniors and come from all over Manitoba and neighboring states and provinces.

Along with managing her business, Evelyn is involved in the Canadian Cancer Society endorsed *Look Good… Feel Better Program* which she modestly admits she was instrumental in bringing to Manitoba in 1992. Evelyn also teaches Continuing Education on hair loss and alternatives, maintains several business memberships and speaks to women's groups. In 1995, Evelyn won the *Manitoba Home Based Business Award.* Then in 1996, she received the first annual *Look Good… Feel Better Volunteer Recognition for Quality Service Award.* She credits the Women's Business Owners Association of Manitoba and the Federal Business Development Bank for her training.

Evelyn's advice: "Know yourself, know your limitations, but keep working at your dream. You will surely find the way."

1998 Update: In late 1997, Evelyn succeeded in having provincial taxes eliminated on wigs purchased because of hair loss or medical treatments. She is now working to have federal taxes removed for these prostheses, and to have them covered under the Manitoba provincial health plan.

Steadfast Values

Barbara Slater
Barb's Buns
Ganges
Salt Spring Island, BC
V8K 2L3

Barb Slater's *Barb's Buns* bakery and coffee shop is a successful entrepreneurial business on Salt Spring Island. Originally a bartender in the remote Queen Charlotte Islands, Barb moved to Salt Spring in the 1980's with two motivations: to provide good bread for her family, and to stay home with her two children. Her mother came and taught her to make simple, homemade bread. Soon Barb was baking bread for all her family, i.e., 22 people living communally! Barb then also began baking bread at home and selling it at the local public market.

Monks in the nearby Buddhist monastery discovered Barb's bread through husband Kevin, then a student of that faith. They became steady customers, sending a cook to Barb's home to buy bread for the monastery.

Studying Buddhism herself, Barb developed a deeper motivating force: as well as providing healthy food, she now wanted to create a "right livelihood" for herself and family, and "provide service for all beings." So, Barb leased space in a new building and went into baking six days per week. The consistent high quality of Barb's baking, and other organic food items, soon made *Barb's Buns* one of the town's meeting places.

Barb's pride in her business stems from genuine mutual affection and respect between herself and her staff of 20. This pride is now stronger than ever; her two teenagers and husband Kevin are now members of the staff. Staff turnover is low.

Barb's compassion, and wonderful sense of humor draw people to her. She provides them with a "sparky" nurturing and wit.

Simultaneously raising children and bread, Barb learned motherhood and business by trial and error, with no plans for either. Like most women, Barb provided for her family and her business first, ahead of herself. She now admits that "next time I would take better care of myself, emotionally and physically." Barb laughingly admits she is finally learning to delegate and to organize her business.

Barb advises aspiring women entrepreneurs: "most importantly, trust yourself and your intuitions."

Energy and Enterprise

Rochelle Huppin Fleck
Chefwear Inc.
4 - 833 N. Orleans St.
Chicago, Illinois
60610

"I never planned to do what I am doing, but to be an entrepreneur was always second nature" says Rochelle Huppin Fleck. A veteran of childhood enterprises such as "selling painted rocks, lemonade, cookies, whatever," Rochelle is now the driving force behind Chefwear Inc.

Attending New York's Culinary Institute of America during the mid 80's, Rochelle rebelled at the men's polyester uniforms with which she was issued. She made pants for herself from cotton material. After graduation, it seemed to Rochelle that the restaurant industry needed upgrading of its uniforms. "Chefwear USA" was born.

During a Meals on Wheels charity event in Los Angeles, several pairs of Chefwear's pants were handed out to famous chefs attending the event. "Everyone who saw the pants freaked out, they thought they were so cool... many asked if they could get a pair."

Chefwear Inc. manufactures and sells from Chicago its "unisex culinary apparel for the restaurant and hospitality industry... and also clothes to people who enjoy cooking at home... or who just like to hang out in our fun line of clothes."

Supported by friends excited at the success of the business, and encouraged by her father to advertise, Chefwear grew rapidly "just shooting from the hip." Rochelle simply designed more and more successful items for Chefwear's line. Now debt free, with some 30 employees and a global ambition, Rochelle is working with a CPA firm to develop three, five and ten year business plans for Chefwear Inc.

As Rochelle notes, "Chefwear stays in touch with... the vibes of the industry... remaining avant-garde... always delivering a quality product and standing behind it."

Rochelle advises any aspiring woman entrepreneur "to go with your instinct, you will usually be correct... and always be willing to mentor other women; your kindness will have a way of continually returning to you."

Life-Long Creativity

Jill Fagin
Jillery Inc.
88 East 10th St.
New York, NY
10003

Jill named her company *Jillery* to combine her given name with her passion for "jewelry." She explains, "...I was always making jewelry and ceramics... I turned to the talent I'd had all my life."

As a child, Jill bent old spoons into rings, played on the beach, took shells home and made them into jewelry. Later, after seeing the single earrings she made for herself, people would stop her on the street and ask her if she could "make another." So she made unmatched asymmetrical earrings and sold them.

In the beginning, Jill worked late every night. "My hands were raw," recalls Jill. But the sacrifices were worth it. Today, in her 30s, she has 12 full-time employees and a very successful business, selling to stores all over the world.

Jill notes that hard work alone isn't enough. Products must appeal to a wide range of people. "There's something in my line for everyone." With aluminum as her signature material, Jill's wide range of merchandise includes fashion jewelry and hair ornaments, home accessories such as mirrors, cocktail stirrers, flatware, vases, candlesticks, picture frames, bottle stoppers, Judaica, baby gifts, and pill boxes.

Jillery has been seen in publications like Cosmopolitan, Seventeen, Sports Illustrated, Women's Wear Daily and others. Yet, like most other successful entrepreneurial businesses, Jill's company had "small beginnings." A top department store buyer discovered Jill Fagin's crafts at a street fair—And the rest is history. Jill now has sales reps across the country, in Germany and Japan, and has just opened her own retail store in New York City.

As Jill says, "I turned my crafts to cash."

Failure Not an Option

Janine Wittich
Tattoo Zoo
1215 Wharf St.
Victoria, BC
V8W 1R9

Tattoo Zoo is an excellent example of a "90's" business, with women in non-traditional roles in non-traditional businesses. Tattoo Zoo, with two locations in Victoria, BC, offers tattooing and body-piercing to women and men in attractive, professional atmospheres.

Owners Janine Wittich and husband Doug state that 60-70% of their clientele are women who "decide to get tattoos or body piercings to celebrate rites of passage or to mark special occasions." Their business is supplying new evidence that "women are more in charge of their lives and bodies than ever before."

One client, to mark her progress through cancer therapy, chose a tattoo of a wolf, symbolizing strength.

Tattoo studios are joining the most respectable of Victoria's businesses. Janine and Doug are providing input and expertise to help local health officials and city council members establish industry standards and guidelines. These include educational material for young people to increase their awareness of health issues and safety concerns.

Janine believes her business provides an alternative to "traditional" studios for tattoo/body piercing, elevating it to an art form and a highly acceptable method of contemporary self-expression.

Janine, wishing for a flexible schedule to allow time for family, originally considered a home secretarial service or collection agency. However, when the tattoo business opportunity presented itself, Janine and Doug chose to learn the business, with no business plan, but with the belief that "failure was not an option."

Janine states, "You don't have to know everything, but you have to be willing to learn."

Service, Including House Calls

"Claire Congdon. Mentor, boss, friend. Twenty-five years... Customer Service Excellence."

Claire Congdon
Congdon's Aids to Daily Living
15819 Stony Plain Rd.
Edmonton, Alberta
T5P 3J7

Wouldn't we all like to be introduced that way. Those were the words on the cover of a profile about Claire, submitted to help her win the 1995 Regional Award in the Lifetime Achievement Category of the Canadian Entrepreneur of the Year Awards.

As this is written, Claire, 69, is celebrating 26 years as a medical and home health care supplier. First established in 1970 as the Ostomy Care Centre, Claire's business has expanded to include post-surgical mastectomy care, sports medicine, home health care supplies and aids for the disabled.

While there are now many competitors serving the home health care needs of Northern Alberta, an emphasis on service, including sending consultants on house calls, has helped maintain Claire's clientele.

Although Claire and husband Bill are edging toward retirement, Claire spends up to three days a week at Congdon's. Bill meanwhile spends part of every day at Eco-Medical, the other family business which sells wheel chairs and health care hardware.

Claire has received many awards and considerable recognition for an enterprise which began 25 years ago, when Claire, with four children at home, learning of the need for a personal care service said, "I can do that!"

Quality Care With Experience

*Flo Shiells (right),
Karin Sullivan (l. back),
Barb Cassin (middle),
Marie Gale (l. front)
Focus on Caring Inc.
208 - 525
11th Ave. SW
Calgary, Alberta
T2R 0C9*

Four registered nurses with over a century of experience between them did not let government health care downsizing faze them. They formed a partnership to market their combined nursing skills, taking advantage of excellent mentoring and strong networking resources in their community.

Offering 24-hour 7-day per week on-call service, *Focus on Caring* offers quality care for the elderly. Services include palliative care, assessments and consultation on elder placement, geriatric rehabilitation support, Alzheimer's respite, foot care, pain management and diabetes management. The partners are qualified through the Alberta Registered Nurses Association for almost every kind of nursing care.

The blend of skills and experience possessed by these RNs is also a huge asset. Previously, one partner was an administrator, another a teacher, the third a business woman, and the fourth had political connections. They have neatly divided responsibilities to create a successful, working partnership—Operations, Marketing, Teaching/Outreach and Finance.

Starting in 1994, the business grew to need many sub-contractors, provided by a network of part-time or unemployed nurses. The partners note that as the population continues to age, the demand for their services will continue to grow.

As one partner observed, "We love nursing. It's just in a new setting."

1998 Update: Still specializing in Geriatrics, we also now care for younger clients with degenerative diseases who are unable to be at home. We no longer use subcontractors, but now have employees with a variety of health care skills. Our caregivers continue to supply services 24-hours, 7 days per week and there is a Registered Nurse 'on call' at all times. Our mandate remains the same: To provide high-quality, personalized nursing care to the community.

Personnel Excellence

Marilyn Sinclair
ObjectArts
2500 - 255
Queens Ave.
London, Ontario
N6A 5R8

As a former Branch Manager of an end-user technical training company, with strong skills in that area, it was a natural for Marilyn. With strong family support, she just "jumped in with both feet" to set up her own high-end technical training business.

Now operating in London, Toronto and New York, Marilyn's company specializes in Microsoft training. "We offer you more courses, more full-time instructors, and more ways to get trained than anyone else. With 3130 satisfied students trained from over 400 corporations this year, we can assure you… Satisfaction Guaranteed!" ObjectArts also markets software products such as a data outline control used by programmers.

Marilyn feels that her success in this highly competitive business is due both to her own technical competence, and her ability to build and manage a great team. She also notes that she works with a business plan that is reviewed annually by her Board of Directors.

Marilyn is very proud when she reads comments from the staff that "…they appreciate the opportunities they have been provided with and consider me a strong leader and role model… which means we are on the right track." You reap what you sow. Offer people respect and loyalty and it will come back to you many times over.

Marilyn also participates in a board of community professionals in London. Their purpose is to mentor and seek funding for entrepreneurs. This is a valuable and natural extension of her business talent.

Her long-term vision for her business is "…to continue growing and motivating young talent and providing a productive, challenging and pleasant work environment for them." As Marilyn notes: "Being an entrepreneur can be a very rewarding and exciting experience but you have to strongly believe in the goals you are trying to achieve and have the perseverance to achieve those goals."

Seniors Education... Labor of Love

Beverly Hincks
Encore Seniors
Education Centre
St. Lawrence College
Cornwall, Ontario
K6H 4Z1

Not all model women entrepreneurs create enterprises with profit objectives. In mid 1993, teacher Beverly Hincks[1] was between teaching contracts when she thought of developing an academic learning program for seniors in her Eastern Ontario community. Bev then spent a year doing demographic studies and needs assessments to present to a local college.

The result was the award-winning *Encore Seniors Education Centre* at St. Lawrence College in Cornwall, Ontario. Encore is a member-led institute, run by Seniors, with Bev as the coordinator.

When Bev learned that her application for funding was approved, in mid-summer 1994, she also learned that it included a part-time job for Bev to organize a program to start in eight weeks! Bev notes the courage of St. Lawrence College in supporting this program during a climate of funding cutbacks. The curriculum includes traditional subjects like history, geography and literature, plus subjects such as native studies, communication, and computer classes. Students can also travel and enjoy learning through affiliated Elderhostel and US based TraveLearn programs.

Encore has received prestigious awards. In 1995, Ontario's Colleges of Applied Arts and Technology bestowed the Conny Award for "Best New Program" in Continuing Education. Also in 1995, the US Association for Continuing Higher Education honored Encore as having the "best new program in North America" in the Older Adult division.

As one senior commented, "Encore is the best thing that ever happened to me. I was vulnerable to loneliness, depression and isolation. Now I meet vibrant new people with a positive outlook on aging and learning."

There is no doubt about the success of Encore. As coordinator Bev notes… "Success… beyond my wildest dreams."

---

[1] The author thanks Mary Van Ryswyk, member of the Encore Advisory Board, whose article in the May/June 1997 Maturity Magazine supplied material about Encore and role model woman entrepreneur Beverly Hincks.

Treasure Your Day Job, Too!

Margaret Huszar
Cat's Meow Creations
104 - 905 Burdett Ave.
Victoria, BC
V8V 3G6

Margaret Huszar comes from a family of ultimate entrepreneurs—farmers. She learned early that "being your own boss involves long hours of blood, sweat and tears, often with little more reward than the satisfaction of doing your own thing."

Margaret always loved working with fabric and her long-held dream was to use fabric in her own designs. She began making ties in the 1970s for her (then) husband, a sales manager, to "set him apart from his competition." At that time, Margaret had a full-time job and three teenagers, so was only able to make ties for friends. However, in 1994, after she herself wore one of her ties and matching vests to work (as a writer at a radio station), the men constantly asked her to make ties for them. That was the start. She began selling her ties in craft circuits, then moved up to trade shows.

Cat's Meow Creations now makes limited edition theme ties and vests—for restaurants, gift shops and other clients in the United States and Canada.

Margaret operates her business on "total honesty, unqualified quality and getting the product to the buyer before the promised date." She also keeps in touch with all her customers on a regular basis—a basic good business skill.

The Cat's Meow creator admitted (in 1996) that it would be "totally frightening to quit my job to go into business full time at this point… but I can see the day when that would be reality… if only I can stop always buying more fabric." Living alone means her work habits don't impact on anyone else, and she receives absolute support from her family and friends.

Her advice to other women: "Go for it! If you have a good idea, a quality product, and can fill a special niche , give it a try. Don't quit your day job for a while. Do some market research. But don't hesitate. Keep a positive attitude and give it a whirl. If you don't, you'll always regret it. Remember, women make the most successful entrepreneurs!"

1998 Update: Margaret is now devoting full-time to her business. While she misses the comfort of paycheques, she now enjoys the extra time she can devote to being open to change. Margaret is experimenting with new products and new fabrics such as hemp/rayon/silk combinations, and now printing many of her designs on these fabrics.

Nineties Niche

Christie Carr
Bureau 2000
International Inc.
118 - 23852
Pacific Coast Hwy.
Malibu, CA 90265

Christie sees herself as a "tireless workaholic who views every new situation as a challenge." Her choice, in 1993, to develop a "900 number service bureau" has turned out to be an excellent decision.

Christie saw, in the burgeoning 900 number industry, a "business opportunities market" niche that she has developed to make her Bureau 2000 International Inc. into a profitable enterprise employing 16 people. Christie's vision for her business sees her expanding in the US, Canada and the "rest of the world."

The "business opportunities market" niche basically provides Christie's clients with all the tools necessary to operate a hands-off business. Popular pay-per-call programs range from psychic, dream interpretation, model and Actline hotline, and adult entertainment, to sports, and custom-designed or exclusive international lines. She has recently produced a 30-minute psychic "infomercial" as well as commercial spots for most of the popular programs offered at Bureau 2000.

Bureau 2000 clients receive everything they need—programming, live operators/actresses to answer their lines, 24-hour service and technical support, and other services.

Christie suggests that, "with no overhead, machinery, inventory or employees, Bureau 2000 is the ideal business for busy executives, students, at-home mothers, or anyone looking for a second source of income."

Her family originally thought "working for others was safer." But as Christie observes, "we all know this is not the case."

Customer Loyalty

Joan Robb
Big Printing Inc.
2814 E. Imperial Highway
Brea, California 92621

Finding it difficult to get a job in 1985, when she was past 40, Joan decided to open *Big Printing*, offering "design capabilities, digital output and two and four-color printing." She chose this business, learning it from the ground floor as she went along, "...because I was good at basic design and with people, and highly intelligent..., and this business was a fit with my background, education and talents."

Since then, Joan has developed a steady customer-servicing business. As she says, "I stay on the leading edge of technology and buy equipment that my customers need." Joan received support in her business venture from her husband, but "always made my own decisions."

Joan works with an overall business plan which is renewed "every year or so." She has encountered no gender-based difficulties; would like to sell the business in about 5 years.

Printing is a demanding and highly competitive business, subject to staff turnover, fickle customers, tardy accounts receivable and consequent working capital problems. Compound that with the California business conditions of the recent past, and you have a tough business in which to survive. Describing herself as a strict but fair employer, Joan has learned over time to adopt a more laissez-faire attitude towards employees. But as Joan says, "We are professionals, here to help our customers succeed... I love what I do, and I'm sure that's what kept me whole during the rough times."

Joan's advice to aspiring women entrepreneurs is "just do what YOU do best."

Communication... at Work

Maureen Betts
Vision Communications
1670 Hillview Cres.
Victoria, BC
V8N 2N5

Maureen Betts is a human relations consultant whose company, Vision Communications, provides mediation services and training programs for educators, professionals, management and employees in government, business and private organizations. Topics include conflict resolution, anger management, assertiveness, bias awareness, and violence prevention. The course, *Women Working Together: Stress Solutions*, focuses on factors that both enhance and threaten work relations among women. Maureen's background includes counseling in psychology and certification in Conflict Resolution and Mediation.

With a life-long interest in human relationships and communication, Maureen knows that collaborative and dispute resolution skills are life skills critical for working productively and effectively together. She believes that people are desperate for these skills in their work and personal lives, and that they are necessary skills for peace in the world.

To provide site-specific training, Maureen assesses the problem(s) a group is having and develops a training program to address it. "I offer a specific course or segments of courses, along with group exercises, demonstrations and coaching that enables participants to work together cooperatively, based on newly learned skills."

Maureen agrees with the research that indicates aggressive behaviors are culturally endorsed and prevalent in both schools and the work place. She feels it is critical that people learn how to handle power struggles constructively and to use communication that is assertive, yet non-defensive, versus a permissive or adversarial approach. Maureen teaches these concepts and skills with passion, in both the educational community and the workplace.

Maureen admits she was fortunate to have had "the luxury of not being self-supporting," allowing her the time and financial independence to do the programming and material designs herself. She worked out of her home, and therefore did not have overhead costs.

Maureen's proudest moments come when "people are inspired at a deep level to make changes in beliefs and attitudes as a result of a training program."

Her advice to other women entrepreneurs: "Remember to use empathy, to always treat others as you wish to be treated," and as importantly, "Don't expect to be an expert. The road to success is always under construction."

Creativity Harnessed

Susan Wright
Artist
Box Q-3, Parkway
Old Chelsea, Quebec
J0X 1N0

After some years of a Bohemian lifestyle in some of life's tougher schools, Susan, now in her mid-thirties with a young daughter to provide for, seems poised to create success for them both in the tough world of fine arts.

Until recently, Susan had applied her life-long creative abilities in a somewhat haphazard style. Then she settled down to work, and raise her child, on British Columbia's sybaritic Salt Spring Island, a haven for many established and struggling artists, artisans and crafts people.

Here, Susan earned a bare living for five years doing odd jobs like sign and house painting, graphic design and, most importantly, portraits of people, animals and particularly, fine horses. Most of the latter work was specifically commissioned, although Susan did create and sell a portfolio of "speculative" pieces on horses and a range of other subjects. A recent piece sold to a member of Canada's National Equestrian Team, giving Susan a great boost to her self-esteem and belief in herself as a professional.

These single-motherhood years on Salt Spring have been a training period for Susan, both for honing largely self-taught artistic talent, and as a time for learning harsh words like strategies, objectives, marketing, self-promotion, and competition. Susan now understands that she is... In Business For Herself... and facing some special problems inherent in this business, i.e. she is the sole producer of her marketable product. Given demand for her work, she cannot simply clone herself or hire more people. Thus, issues like market targets, self-promotion, bread-and-butter art pieces, pricing, time-management, her own health and budgets are new realities.

For family and economic reasons, Susan has now returned to her home in the province of Quebec. With improved security, some serendipitous studio arrangements, and a clearer artistic and business vision, Susan is starting almost all over again. But with optimism and positive thinking, her own innate talent, her clear new focus, and the luck often created from sheer hard work, Susan is going to do fine.

As Susan says, "Setting new higher standards for myself and, with positive new visualizations, is the fuel which gets me over the hurdles and on to greater goals."

18

Empowering Self-Strategies

By this time, you will be "up to here" with advice, information, suggestions, sources of more information, etc. It will be academic unless you use it. It's up to you to **take action**. Perhaps some final reinforcement will help.

You have read this book, and perhaps others like it, because you know you must make a change. Not that your current life is bad, but you know that more is possible in your life and you are sure you have the potential.

The question is: what can you do with your life, to create greater meaning for you? For things to get better for you, you must get better. Life improves by making changes, not by chance. You are responsible for your world. Unless you take responsibility for what's going on, nothing will change.

Look for people who have the results you want and do the same things. Be specific about what you want, because if you focus long and hard, you'll get what you focus on. As one wise adage puts it, "you'll see it when you believe it." If you can help others define what they want, and help them get it, then you will get what you want.

You must commit yourself 100% to whatever you undertake. If you give 100% of yourself, you have achieved success, regardless of what else happens. Giving 100% is your way of acknowledging that there is always a way to achieve your goal, that you have cut off any other result but success. So there are no failures, just stepping stones to success as **you** define it.

In wishing you all that you wish for yourself and your important others, you are urged to focus on these powerful thoughts:

If you can't, then you must. – Anthony Robbins

Action is the real measure of intelligence.
– Napoleon Hill, from "Think and Grow Rich"

It's a funny thing about life. If you refuse to accept anything but the best, you very often get it. – W. Somerset Maugham

and my favorite:

Fragrance lingers on hands that give roses. – Anonymous

On This Day

Mend a quarrel
Search out a forgotten friend
Dismiss suspicion, and replace it with trust
Write a love letter
Share some treasure
Give a soft answer
Encourage youth
Manifest your loyalty in a word or deed
Keep a promise
Find the time
Forego a grudge
Forgive an enemy
Listen
Apologize if you are wrong
Try to understand
Flout envy
Examine your demand on others
Think first of someone else
Appreciate, be kind, be gentle
Laugh a little more
Deserve confidence
Take up arms against malice
Decry complacency
Express your gratitude
Worship your God
Gladden the heart of a child
Take pleasure in the beauty and wonder of the earth
Speak your love
Speak it again
Speak it still again
Speak it still once again

– Unknown

19

More Role Models — Brief Stories

Detail or identities have been avoided in these vignettes, but each one illustrates a point. One of the less obvious lessons is that the enterprise does not have to be enormous, just successful—as the entrepreneur defines that.

The hope is that you will find one special example, one which makes you stare off into a space that only you can see, and say quietly to yourself, and to the world, "Yes—I could do that—maybe better—why not!" And there you'll be, about to—**take action**.

1 Margo is one of San Francisco's important caterers. Her customers are a Who's Who of celebrities and VIPs. There's talk of cook books, radio and TV shows. Margo was blessed with parents who told her "she could do anything she wanted." She chose to try catering on her own and invested $150 in fancy business cards. Her godfather, a caterer for whom she had once worked, helped land a Christmas party for an important celebrity. She's never looked back, now employs 30 people and is so busy, she can be selective about taking on new clients. Margo was 18, a first-year college student, when she started her (now) very successful catering business.

2 Terri walks dogs, changes kitty litter, waters plants, feeds/brushes pets and forwards mail for absent homeowners. She chose to provide simple, services so she could be at home to raise her daughter. House calls average 30 minutes, and she builds business by referrals. Terri gets good results from classified ads in a local women's magazine. Terri and her daughter know that this business suits them both fine.

3 Sixty representatives across the country now handle Erline's natural skin care products. Starting with $200, half of it borrowed, she had a factory make up private label lipsticks and nail polish. Then she developed eye and lip pencils, and foundation cream. Erline eventually quit her job to get into the cosmetics business full time. But prudently, she looked for a long while before she leapt.

4 Trixie has good taste and listens well. This enables her to buy clothes, shoes, or gift accessories for other people, to offer genuine service. Trixie helps "put things together," something not everyone is able to do.

Clients include advertising agencies as well as individuals. Tact is essential—Sometimes Trixie has to tell people that some things are wrong for them.

5 To subsidize her regular job, Ellen put out flyers in an upscale area offering estate sitting. Someone with an ailing rose garden called. Ellen studied a book on roses and brought the ailing ones back to health. She advertises in local newspapers and travels by bike, along with her trusty hand clippers, pruners and trowel. Ellen now designs and plants patio gardens eight months a year. Business is great—more than she can handle.

6 Rhoda's four-year old company provides figure and style analysis, wardrobe planning, closet audit, make up and skin care, and color analysis. She also offers classes in scarf tying and exercise. Her initial investment of under $1,000 bought her the training and the necessary equipment. Rhoda advertised in a community monthly, and spread the word at professional associations. She's an avid believer in networking. You can't always predict what combination of services will work together.

7 Mercy started her cleaning company on almost no money at all. She circulated 500 flyers a few times in neighborhoods close to her. The phone just started ringing. She enlisted her own housekeeper, and then her daughter as the first cleaning crew, then hired more. Customers provide the cleaning supplies. Mercy had herself and her staff bonded.

8 Helping put people's stressed-out daily lives in order provides a nice business for Glenda and partner, Margaret. They balance checkbooks, find odd-sized clothing, organize rooms or closets, shop for groceries, pick up dry-cleaning and fill unusual requests. One time they had to find a molar for a client who wanted to give it as a gift. They started with business cards, a phone, a copier and ads in their city's magazine. Word of mouth now brings them clients from all over their metro area. Glenda and Margaret work as much or as little as suits them.

9 In smart-looking boutiques, and at large discounts, Karina sells consignment clothes for kids. Parents are paid cash for the clothing which must be in top shape. With the help of her husband, Karina now has revenues in the $7 million a year range.

10 Julie runs a home-based business where a bride-to-be can purchase a "new to her" gown in perfect condition. Julie's husband remodeled the lower level of their home to create a businesslike salon area, complete with chandeliers. It's a business that gives huge satisfaction even though it

may not promise huge wealth. Julie sells on consignment, divides proceeds 50:50 with the former owner and when she sends the check, tells the former owner something about the new owner. Sharing the new owner's joy with the former owner of the dress doubles Julie's pleasure.

11 Martha and Cora help pre-schoolers become comfortable with computer technology. They began by buying a computer to tutor three to five year-olds in a variety of subjects, from programming to art to math. They are now ready to franchise.

12 After working as an English teacher, but never at newspapers, Lisa bought her hometown weekly newspaper. Overnight, Lisa became editor, publisher and sole editorial employee. Making an investment in sophisticated desktop publishing computer equipment and programs, Lisa learned, very quickly, how to put out a newspaper.

13 Do you take visitors to your bookstore for a good time? Then you don't live in the city that claims one of the largest independent bookstores in the nation. And one of the most loved. Sandra's multi-story book store offers some 100,000 titles, and has some 300,000 volumes in inventory. Sofas abound, chairs are plentiful, to help with the cozy informal atmosphere. Part of the secret of Sandra's success is the thorough two-week training she insists upon for all new employees, even those who are part-time. She stresses building trust with customers as the basis of creating customer support. Her approach works.

14 Ethel makes napkin rings and other ceramic items. Starting by baking items in her oven and painting them with nail polish, Ethel quickly sold everything she could make. So she bought a mini-model kiln, taught herself to use it, and got serious about her ceramics business. For a change of pace from napkin rings, Ethel makes picture frames, Christmas ornaments and jewelry. Ethel's start-up costs were for nail polish and lacquer. She made her own business cards. That's a low cost start-up!

15 Having just been laid off from her job, Susan got the idea of a catering business. She scribbled pages of notes, went to the library for research, enrolled in a 10-week business development course at a local university, brain-stormed with trusted friends, and was soon on her way. Her company offers food preparation geared to parties. And they clean up afterwards, too. In the second bedroom of her apartment, she has her phone, fax and computers. Her mother, Irene, works closely with Susan,

helping her to set up and to cook. Husband Charles is the taste tester. Her classic approach to researching her business is paying off.

16 Deirdre runs a market research and consulting firm that also publishes books and newsletters. Her office is in a spare bedroom. Because she often works weekends, every Friday night is "date night" with her husband of 23 years. Deirdre believes in professional routine, and dresses for business, even when she's at home.

> **Make New Friends**
>
> You can make more new friends in two months by becoming really interested in other people than you can in two years by trying to get other people interested in you.
>
> — Dale Carnegie

She is also a believer in planning and networking. She joined a number of business groups, becoming a committee member or officer in all of them. High visibility is valuable for promoting business. Volunteering for community service projects put Deirdre in contact with business leaders and allowed her to build personal credibility. Networking is so important!

17 Gail has beaten the colossal odds against success in the restaurant business. Customers are genuinely welcomed at her restaurants and line up to get in. But instead of franchising, Gail has elected to keep control and expand more slowly, at least for awhile. She sees further opportunities, such as a "general store" at each restaurant; possibly a mail-order business selling specialized southern restaurant goodies.

Personal passion for the business is what's needed. Gail's management style of deliberately inviting input from employees in operating decisions is most effective. In a business notorious for staff turnover, Gail has many employees who have stayed with her since the restaurants opened. Strategies like quality, service, employee involvement and commitment, steady control of expansion, are basic and they keep paying off.

18 Though Maria wished she had more business training, she learned on the job when she opened up her Italian store featuring a cheese and meat deli, freshly made Italian salads and pastas, and Italian wines.

Maria's family have been supportive. Husband Tony provided marketing expertise, started food shopping and became an excellent cook at home. Both of her children worked in the store after school and on weekends.

Maria expanded into a second, very much larger location, but has resisted further expansion. As she puts it, each location needs her hands-on participation. An integral part of Maria's "luck" is the loving support from her family. She found that the harder she worked, the luckier she became.

19 Tracy feels that direct mail is one of the ways to succeed with businesses in out-of-the-way places. This is how she rescued her isolated store selling preserved and arranged dried flowers and herbs.

Tracy wanted a home-based cottage industry: no commuting, no office wardrobe, no baby sitting, and to be at home with her young son. So she converted the front of her restored 18th century house. She wrapped the store in wallpapers and chintz, antique fixtures, lace-trimmed cloths and baskets of dried flowers and herbs.

Advertising in the adjacent city, Tracy helped turn her community into a tourist center. She encouraged a dozen other stores to sell antiques and collectibles, all attracting weekenders from the city and many interstate highway travelers as well.

But, frustrated with the hectic summer pace versus the deadly quiet winter, Tracy decided that a catalog would bring the store to customers in their homes at times when they would not come to the store. After some classic mistakes, Tracy's mail order business is profitable and growing, and her store is thriving, too. Sometimes the only way to go is to jump right in.

20 When Jane first opened her literary agency some 15 years ago, she had a makeshift office in her city apartment, no capital, no staff and only ten authors, all unpublished. Now, her gross sales are in the millions, and she has sold for hefty advances several novels that she expects to see on best-seller lists.

Like many other small business owners, her problem is one of growth. As demand for her services expands, she cannot meet the demand for her skills. And on behalf of her authors, she's a tough negotiator, which prompts deep loyalty from her now 80-plus writers.

To deal with growth, Jane had to delegate some of the tasks she was handling. Jane stays motivated by only representing authors to which she was committed. She either believes in authors or she doesn't take them on, seeing herself as a career partner with each author.

By dividing and delegating, but keeping what she loves doing best, Jane continues to prove that passion pays.

21 Not all entrepreneurs are young, or work as we know it. Mary, 78, recently set off from Newfoundland in a sturdy, well-found double-end sloop, to sail to Ireland. Eleanor, 79, bent almost double from spinal osteoporosis fractures, and using a walker, averaged 10 walking miles per day and visited over 80 communities in a series of walks across Canada to draw

attention to osteoporosis. It took her and some stalwart teammates four and a half months the first year to cross from Vancouver, on the West Coast, to Toronto. She completed the Toronto to East Coast leg the second year.

22 Erin, boss of a recycling company, thinks that women are their own worst enemies when it comes to getting into business. "Women believe that the business world is going to be too much for them. They must overcome that attitude." Erin's conviction calls for vision, determination, self-confidence and a willingness to learn. Using these, Erin has built a company that collects, sorts and grades recyclable material. She sells the recycled material to companies which turn glass, plastic, newspapers and cans into usable products, employs 120 people, and can claim sales of some $10 million. As a winner of entrepreneurial awards, Erin points out that "women are a major force that can't be stopped, so you might as well welcome us with open arms."

23 Some hobbies just grow and grow, and suddenly there's this super little business. Agnes persuaded four friends to join her in a course to make "chocolate things." When the course was over, her four friends relaxed from chocolate. Not Agnes. With her husband bravely cranking out tin molds in his workshop, Agnes soon had trouble giving away all the "chocolate things" she was making. Sending quantities to school for her kids to give away, the inevitable happened. Someone asked her to supply quantities to sell. Agnes is now really busy making chocolate things. Her husband is pleased, too. He has some new tools for molds and he enjoys managing the growing cash flow, even though he still seldom eats chocolate.

24 One enterprising woman whose name I don't know, saw an opportunity to give tourists a comfortable, safe ocean ride between two or three easily reached scenic harbors (one of which features a nice waterfront pub). This lady had a unique boat designed and built locally. Two hulls (catamaran style) provide a stable platform that is easy to move through the sheltered and safe waters. But the genius of the design is that it can be driven by a couple of easily serviced outboard engines. She laughs at operating costs, and if an engine needs service, she just pops on a spare. She is on the sea, cash is up front, she is busy and she looks healthy and happy.

25 Sharon, while on welfare, responded to an advertised offer for computer/word processing training. She was one of a large group who turned up to apply and for whom there turned out to be no space in the class. Thinking quickly, Sharon announced to the disappointed throng, that she would provide the computer/word processing training. Just leave names

and addresses and she'd be in touch. And so she was. She hired an instructor, rented space and opened for business. Sharon's training and development center blossomed. She's thinking of franchising.

26 With experience as a day-care center employee, and frustrated in her search for educational toys for her youngsters, Beth founded her toy-importing company. Working from her garage, she tried home parties. This worked and Beth now has toy consultants selling toys in the US, Canada and Japan. The company is expanding overseas and going into children's quilts and wallpaper. This business is serious fun.

27 Hannah's travel agency was doing fine but she knew it could do better if she marketed more aggressively. Taking advice from her mentor who had lots of relevant experience in using trade shows, Hannah started working this medium. And from her mentor, she learned how to choose her location, how to staff and operate her display booth, and how to employ distinctive colors in her booth design to catch the fleeting attention of passersby. Along with some catchy free draw promotions, business has boomed as a result of trade show activities.

28 As Francine notes, "I had to re-think my hibernation instinct." In order to promote her company, a program of networking was somewhat reluctantly adopted by Francine. She joined the local Chamber, a council on the status of women, did volunteer work and participated in church work and political activities. Everywhere she went, she gave out business cards, then followed up with phone calls. There is often no hard line between business and socializing, and networking never stops!

29 Nothing prepared Nancy for the blitz of paperwork involved in administering her heating, air conditioning and plumbing company. She bought a computer but was afraid to use it. Her mentor put her in touch with a computer consultant who installed a business management program and taught her how to use it.

Now Nancy learns, on a daily basis the cost/status of each project. The program has helped Nancy's company achieve profits in year two. It does pay to know how you are doing.

30 Pat needed to provide for her son and herself, after a marriage break-up. Fortunately, her homemade tomato sauce recipe was so popular, people were asking to be able to buy it in case lots. After a presentation to a chain of upscale grocery stores, they took her product.

Now needing to produce her recipe in quantity, Pat could not find a co-packer (a company that makes product for you) who would produce her recipe. Passionately on a mission, she went to a nearby university lab for instructions on how to do her recipe and comply with food-safety guidelines.

She took long drives to buy good produce, parking her tiny car among tractor trailers. With incredible family support, Pat produced and delivered her first order. Before she knew it, orders were coming from other gourmet food shops in her area.

Pat soon ran out of working capital. After enormous struggles the family run ragged simply producing the sauce—She knew she needed help.

Pat formed a partnership with a specialty food company. Retaining control of her company, Pat is now working out the happier problems of big production facilities.

A strong need, passionate belief, sturdy family and friends, huge obstacles, unquenchable determination, Pat's story illustrates classic entrepreneurial endeavor. You can just hear the tractor trailer drivers as they watched her stuff tomatoes into her tiny car—But you better believe she had their sincere respect.

31 Comical encounters are commonplace for Daphne. Recently, when on an airplane, she opened her case to feed mulberry leaves to voracious silk worms. Fellow passengers stared, thinking she was making a bizarre salad.

Daphne has been raising silk worms for years. The only problem is that in the feeding stage, they must be fed every two hours. After about a month, they stop eating and begin spinning. Daphne dyes their gossamer threads, spins them, weaves them and creates gorgeous shimmering garments.

32 Louise is a talented vocalist and a magical storyteller. To embellish her stories, she used to make puppets out of household recyclable "throw-aways" for use at her children's birthday parties. Inevitably, she was offered fees to come and do other birthday parties. Eventually, this led to special puppet and storytelling performances on now internationally syndicated TV programs. A large part of Louise's success is the result of a true marriage partnership, where her husband, George, has been her business manager and partner from the earliest days.

Don't let anyone spoil your dreams.

– Terrell Davis, Denver Broncos,
MVP, 1998 Superbowl

33 In Robin's business, when the soil moves, it's eating garbage. Tens of thousands of garbage-chewing red wriggly worms have changed Robin's life, and helped her create a thriving business. Vermi-composting is the name for the process where busy red worms happily chew garbage and turn it into a first-class soil additive. Robin now supplies wrigglers and composting bins to many garden supply shops, who in turn sell kits to home owners. These are often apartment or townhouse dwellers who don't have conventional gardens and compost heaps. Once or twice a week, food waste of an astonishing variety (no garlic or onions though!) is buried in the bins. As it decomposes, the worms transform it into high grade manure, rich in nutrients and safe for all plants.

Robin feels that worm composting, then growing some of your own food, is a way of becoming connected with the earth—an attractive concept.

34 A small town in British Columbia's Shuswap area is now open again. An enterprising lady and her cat moved there from Vancouver, to become the town's only inhabitants. They re-opened the general store which had been run by previous owners from 1927 to 1982. The new owner also expanded the available habitable space by adding three railway cabooses. These were converted into living space for her backpackers' hostel. This works well because the area is attractive for camping, boating, river rafting, cross-country skiing, and sockeye salmon watching. Quite a career change for this young lady, who had recently worked as an interior designer.

35 Essential oils can relieve headaches, rid animals of fleas and keep aphids off roses. There is an incredible range of uses for the hundreds of essential oils found in some flowers, herbs, spices and trees.

Two young retailers, Marsha and Gwen, recently opened a modern apothecary offering a two-way approach to their vast selection of essential oils. You may buy pre-blended shampoos, face and body lotions, massage oils and bath products, or you may shop for "recipes" in the store's source books, then buy the ingredients to make up your own applications.

Marsha, a former financial consultant, and Gwen, a registered massage therapist, approach their products with both humor and respect. There is no doubt that Marsha and Gwen are right in tune with the growing emphasis among both men and women on nurturing and wellness.

36 An American company is seeking an overseas partner for a joint venture. Sounds like a case for Janet, a pioneer in global marketing. To help her client, Janet phoned an associate in Asia. They found a Japanese joint venture partner interested in marketing the product in Asia.

Janet moved into global matchmaking some years ago when she noticed American companies becoming more interested in export markets. Her company devotes over 60% of its time to finding "strategic affiliates," joint-venture partners, overseas marketing representatives and licensing agents.

37 When others are commuting to work, Melanie is already at her home office—her bed. Surrounded by her cellular phone, fax machine, laptop computer and printer, she watches stock market action on her television, and buys and sells accordingly. "I start work at 6, finish at about 9, and then I get up," she says. "It's the only way to go," says this enterprising entrepreneur. "Home offices are the way of the future, and soon everyone is going to catch on to that fact."

38 When Sylvia's husband died she was left with two children, large debts, and the certainty that a nine to five job would simply not provide enough. After a friend talked about a successful scrap metal business, Sylvia realized she could do that, despite never having had a serious entrepreneurial thought up to that point in her life.

Driving a rented truck down alleys, cold-calling at back doors of businesses, scrounging scrap metal wherever she could find it, Sylvia developed a clientele. Eventually, she built a sophisticated company, a company strongly contributing to recycling and environmental issues in her community.

39 Wendy is clear on her five-year goal. "I want to work with women who have their journeyman carpenter's papers." Wendy has been working on this since she was a child. Fixing things, carpentry, and painting woodwork were activities Wendy and her mother did with pride.

Following a stint as a bookkeeper, Wendy, as one of three women, enrolled in an apprenticeship course for cabinet making. The first year was spent building galley kitchens for pleasure boats. She now works in partnership with another contractor sharing facilities and tools. Wendy is finding a niche for her skill. "The woman homeowner often feels more comfortable with me because I'm also a woman," says Wendy. With the numbers of women purchasing homes, her goal is within sight.

40 Bonnie and husband, Robin, home-make healthy, frozen fruitcicles from yogurt and fresh, local fruits and berries, then sell them in local and off-island fairs and festivals. This hot-weather business succeeds so well that Bonnie and Robin welcome the off-season slowdown. At last though, Bonnie, who is a fine-arts graduate, is giving more of her energy and creativity to her art, the work she loves best. She is enjoying considerable success in the sale of her paintings, cards and prints.

20

The Virtues Project

Introduction

This particular role model woman entrepreneur story, of Linda Kavelin Popov and her "Virtues Project," is presented separately from the other stories for two reasons. First it is not really a 'business' story, although it is being run on business guidelines for its global financing and application. Second, it is simply such a different and enormous role model woman entrepreneur story; an extraordinary project driven by one woman's passion to help improve the world.

Linda's story is an example of the kind of compassionate global mission and success that is possible. It makes me believe that my personal dream, in the next chapter, is also possible and realistic.

Global Idealism and Vision

How can we combine our talents to serve the planet?

This majestic question was considered by Linda Kavelin Popov and her family over breakfast one morning in April, 1988. Please read the question again. Savor it, as I did.

Linda Kavelin Popov
The Virtues Project Inc.
Box 240, Ganges PO
Salt Spring Island, BC
V8K 2V9

Linda, husband Dan, and brother John Kavelin, concluded that if they could empower children and adults to live by their highest values, the world could be changed in two generations. Their mission is service; profit was not a major objective. Nevertheless, The Virtues Project founders have met with great success through the sales of their books, materials, lectures, seminars.

The Family Virtues Guide first self-published by the Linda Kavelin-Popov family in 1991, is the basic element of the project, teaching children and adults moral qualities common to great religions—52 virtues such as kindness, courage, truth and tolerance. By 1996, The Family Virtues Guide was translated into 15 languages; more than 60,000 copies of The Family Virtues Guide were sold—by word of mouth alone.

As Linda says, "...people appreciate the fact that there is no hidden religious agenda. [The book] helps people re-connect with spirituality they already have. The guide deals with principles of spiritual parenting; how to set clear boundaries for a child; what is the appropriate use of authority. It encourages you to see your child as a champion who has gifts within."

In 1994, during the International Year of the Family, The Virtues Project was honored by the UN Secretariat and World Conference of Cities and Corporations as "a model global program for families of all cultures." The program is taught by some 2,000 facilitators, trained by Linda and husband Dan, to parents groups, social workers, physicians and care-givers around the globe. Not just for parenting, The Family Virtues Guide is used with street kids in Seattle; for rehabilitation in penitentiaries in British Columbia, Texas and Australia; with school violence prevention programs in American cities; in healing programs for Canadian First Nations communities; and as a text with instructive cultural values for those studying English. A major strength of the project is that it is producing sincere personal commitments from individuals who want to be involved, both for the sake of their families and for the planet.

To meet the growing global demand, Linda will train facilitator-trainers to expand the program, but only "with integrity." The demand is intensifying. In 1997, Penguin published *The Family Virtues Guide* and Linda's new book, *Sacred Moments: Daily Meditations on the Virtues* (see quotation from this book, on page 77).

Linda and her associates in The Virtues Project are carrying forth an awe-inspiring global project, with incalculable humanitarian potential.

Linda's advice to other women entrepreneurs: "Follow your heart. What is your biggest dream? Dare to discern it and ask for Divine help. Then watch what happens!"

1998 Update: Linda Kavelin Popov and her inspiring book, *The Family Virtues Guide* were recently featured on the Oprah Winfrey show.

21

A Dream

We all need dreams. My dream is to have a tiny influence on helping our planet be at peace, enjoying sustaining practices for all matter and creatures; a world better for my grandchildren, theirs—and yours.

The world now needs compassion, education about its condition, volunteers in the millions, and all of us committed to bringing about crucial adjustments to distribute wealth more fairly; to manage resources; and perhaps most importantly, to be willing to start making the adjustments necessary for environmental repairs.

I now believe that considerable hope for recognizing and working towards meeting these needs lies with women entrepreneurs, as a result of their capabilities and characteristics, as outlined in the Prologue and Chapter One of this book.

Only as a grandfather have I had the wisdom to note and study these qualities of women. They are powerful revelations and have inspired this book—which lets me feel that I am finally carrying out some of my responsibilities to my five grandchildren.

I wish to encourage women to maximize their entrepreneurial power. For example, as a woman entrepreneur, **you** might start as a leader in some local environmental or humanitarian work. If that is as far as you want to take it, that's fine; you are making an important contribution.

But who knows, perhaps you will feel a bigger role evolving for yourself, on a larger stage.

The Leader, and Her Leaders

World-wide, women entrepreneurialism flourishes. Within this movement, a new woman leader will emerge, a female Martin Luther King. She will come from the grassroots; an entrepreneur, perhaps one of the role models in this book. **She will understand power and influence.**

> *If we don't change direction, we'll end up where we're headed.*
>
> – Chinese Proverb

The genius of this visionary will be her ability to identify, develop and organize the work of other local and regional leaders. Leaders who will begin uniting the already colossal, and growing, economic, cultural, social, financial and political power being developed by entrepreneurial women all over the world. She will see her visions; other women will see that she sees them, and want to join her. Could this be you?

Initial Financing

Work of the scale envisioned will require money, lots of it. Fortunately, there are corporations in North America with vision, wisdom and acumen. They will recognize that supporting woman-inspired movements which address world social and environmental issues will identify with their own objectives.

Corporations will study these movements and cautiously commence investing. The merits of "sponsorship" will become evident to more and more corporations as they become aware of the strength and power of these grassroots humanitarian networks.

Volunteers

From where do we recruit dedicated volunteers… to plan, train, teach, clean, medicate, plant, inspire, write, sing, govern, fund-raise… etc?

The answer is among young people; millions of parents who share concern about the world for their children; countless other young people now participating in worthy causes. They will all rejoice in movements dedicated to improving their world.

Another source of volunteers is the thousands of athletes from myriad countries who compete at the Olympics and other international games. Can you think of more dedicated, committed groups of people to draw from? People with cultural exposure for whom joyous new commitments to world health and peace could be absolutely right. People we can identify; people with whom we can communicate.

One person can make a difference.

People needn't feel that they should try to change the world single-handed. There are many people working on this project. But just because a person can't do everything, doesn't mean they should do nothing.

Government Support

This international crusade, probably blossoming first in North America, should eventually be supported by every tax-paying citizen and corporation in the world.

With government co-operation and second millennium technology, collection of "a little bit from everyone" could be operated efficiently by a sophisticated non-profit Foundation.

This could painlessly generate hundreds of millions of dollars per year, supplementing corporate sponsorship, to fund research, planning, education, recruiting, training and projects world-wide.

Communications

Global communications will be required to create awareness, encourage the appearance of leaders, volunteers and funding. Although world events attracting simultaneous audiences of this magnitude are not common, the various international Games, hosted periodically all over the world, could fill this vital marketing and communication need.

With enlightened corporate support, Games could provide the media platform and international goodwill, from which to deliver messages, in their own languages, to billions of television viewers… messages inviting participation in world-wide humanitarian and environmental initiatives.

Conclusion

In my dream, responsible citizens, led by women entrepreneurs, will finally grasp that the consequences of not improving environmental and humanitarian conditions in the world are unacceptable… either for my grandchildren… or theirs.

Leaders will emerge. Enlightened business sponsors will invest. Governments will make funding resources possible.

Heartened young people all over the world will volunteer, believing that, at long long last, their elder peers have finally become serious about improving the condition of our planet.

This is my dream. What is yours?

David Bryn-Jones
Salt Spring Island, British Columbia, Canada
July 1998.

I believe in the ability of one person to change the world.

– Julia Payson, Okanagan, BC, high school student, winner of a Canada Trust Scholarship for Outstanding Community Leadership.

Index to Appendices

Introduction to Appendices

Gathering Information

Planning an entrepreneurial endeavor is, to a great degree, an orderly, methodical gathering and processing of information. The process is designed to help make practical and possible the entrepreneurial dream, or to illustrate why the dream has flaws.

The easiest thing for the creative imagination to do is to daydream of the incredible success that is naturally to follow the brilliant idea. That is quite fine, if there is also an awareness of the realities. As someone said, it usually requires a great deal of time and work to create the overnight success story.

Appendix I and II present some of the sources available to you for answering questions and gathering information for the US and for Canada.

Answering Tough Questions

The workbook section in Appendix III is to give you at least some of the key questions you need to answer as you create your future. Answering them is not a simple matter. You may want to consult others. Real honesty is required, not only from you, but also from any others from whom you will truly accept advice.

There will be huge satisfaction though, when you work through all the questions. You will find that either what you've been considering stands careful scrutiny, or you are saved from a dangerous adventure.

Look at the process positively. You can't lose. If your project is good, you have a very promising beginning. If it's not, you will have been fortunate to find out in time. And look how experienced you will be to go through the process again (and maybe even again) to look at other visions.

Whichever way you look at this tough, demanding homework, **you** are the beneficiary. **Go for it!**

APPENDIX I

Sources of Information in the US

The place to start when seeking information and assistance for new and small business, in all 50 states, is the Federal Small Business Administration (SBA).

1. Small Business Answer Desk

US Small Business Administration
409 3rd Street SW, 5th Floor
Washington, DC 20416

The Small Business Answer Desk helps callers with questions on how to start and manage a business, where to get financing, and a wide variety of other specialized information needed to operate and expand a business. A toll-free hotline is provided by SBA's Office of Advocacy. The above address can be used wherever SBA is referred to in the following.

2. Directory of Federal and State Business Assistance

National Technical Information Service
US Department of Commerce
5285 Port Royal Road
Springfield, VA 22161

The Directory of Federal and State Business Assistance describes federal and state programs designed to help new companies compete in domestic and international markets. The directory includes how to get funding for a company's research and development, where to get mail lists of potential overseas business buyers, who provides venture money, and what federal and state contacts offer free management consulting.

3. Federal Money for Business

Federal funds, consulting and training available to small businesses, entrepreneurs, inventors and researchers are outlined in the Catalog of Federal Domestic Assistance, published by the US Government Printing Office in Washington, DC. See also Careers and Workplace; Research Grants in Every Field

Some specific programs:

- Loans for Small Business:
  Director, Loan Policy Branch, SBA
  For small businesses owned by low-income persons in areas of high unemployment.
- Small Business Investment Companies:
  Director, Office of Investments, SBA
  To establish privately-owned and managed small business investment companies; to provide equity capital, long-term funds and advisory services.
- Small Business Loans:
  Director, Loan Policy and Procedures Branch, SBA
  To provide loans to small businesses unable to obtain financing in the private marketplace, but which demonstrate an ability to repay loans granted.
- Service Corps of Retired Executives:
  National SCORE Office
  1825 Connecticut Avenue NW
  Washington, DC 20009
  To use the experience of retired and active business executives; to counsel and train potential and existing small businesses; to be the primary SBA source of one-on-one business counseling.
- Women's Business Ownership:
  Office of Women's Business Ownership, SBA
  To promote the legitimate interest of small business concerns owned and controlled by women.

4. Small Business Innovative Research Programs (SBIR)

The SBIR stimulates technological innovation, encourages small science and technology-based firms to participate in government-funded research, and provides incentives for converting research results into commercial applications. Firms should contact:

Office of Innovation, Research and Technology
Small Business Association
1441 L Street, NW, Washington, DC.

5. The Best Place to Start to Sell To The Government

Within each state there are places to contact to obtain help in getting started in the federal procurement process. The local Small Business Administration office can provide a list of federal procurement offices in your state. Other places are your local Small Business Development Center, under Economic Development in the phone book. Procurement Assistance Offices (PAOs) assist businesses with defense procurement.

- **Let Your Elected Representative Help You**
  Are you trying to market a product to the government? Your elected representatives can be of assistance. They want business in their constituency to boom, so they will make an effort to assist companies in obtaining federal contracts. For your Representative's phone numbers, call (202)224-3121.
- **Small Business Set-Asides**
  The SBA encourages government purchasing agencies to set aside suitable purchases for exclusive small business competition, identified by a set-aside clause in the invitation for bids on requests for proposals. A small business learns which purchases are reserved for small business by getting listed on bidders' lists and by referring to the Commerce Business Daily. Your local SBA office can provide you with more information on set-asides.
- **Woman-Owned Business Assistance**
  Government policy requires federal officers to increase purchases from women-owned businesses. The women-owned firms still must be the lowest responsible bidder to win the contract. To assist these businesses, each SBA district office has a Women's Business Representative. Most offices hold a *Selling to the Federal Government* seminar, designed to educate the business owner on government procurement. A helpful publication, *Women Business Owners: Selling to the Federal Government*, provides

information on the opportunities available. Contact your local SBA office for more information.

6. Basic Guide to Exporting

This publication outlines steps to determine how to use foreign markets. It provides a guide to appraising sales potential of foreign markets and to understanding foreign business practices and procedures. Available from:

Superintendent of Documents
US Government Printing Office
Washington, DC 20402

- *Exporter's Guide to Federal Resources for Small Business*
  Available free from any of the SBA field offices or contact:
  Office of International Trade, SBA
- *Market Overseas with US Government Help*
  Describes agencies of the federal government which offer programs to assist businesses involved in international trade. Available from the SBA, Box 30, Denver, CO 80201.
- *Commercial News USA*
  Describes a free export promotion service that will publicize the availability of your new product to foreign markets, and test foreign market interest in your new product. There is a small fee.
  Marketing Programs Section
  Room 2106
  US Department of Commerce
  Washington, DC 20320
- *ABCs of Exporting*
  This is a special issue of Business America which goes step by step through the exporting process. Free from Trade Information Center, US Department of Commerce, Washington, DC 20230.

7. Small Business Investment Companies (SBIC)

Finance and Investment Division, SBA

SBA licenses and provides financial assistance to privately-owned small business investment companies. Their function is to make venture investments by supplying equity capital and extending unsecured loans and loans not fully collateralized to small enterprises which meet their investment criteria. (See Women's Collateral World-Wide Inc., page 61)

8. Solar Energy and Conservation Loans

Contact your local SBA office or the Small Business Answer Desk. Financial assistance is provided to small business concerns engaged in the engineering, manufacturing, distributing, marketing, installing, or servicing of energy measures designed to conserve the Nation's energy resources.

9. Starting and Managing a Business From Your Home

Superintendent of Documents
US Government Printing Office
Washington, DC 20402

The publication, *Starting and Managing a Business From Your Home*, provides descriptions of products and services to help you start your home-based business. It includes a questionnaire to help you decide if you are the typical entrepreneur, and also gives helpful information on managing your business, including tips on structure, record-keeping, taxes and insurance.

10. Money, Management and Marketing

Business Initiative, Education and Training, SBA

Focus on the Facts is a series of information sheets as listed below. To obtain copies, contact the office above.

- How to Raise Money for a Small Business
- How to Start a Small Business
- Planning… The Most Important Ingredient
- Knowing your Market
- Information… The Key to Success
- How to Price Your Products and Services
- Opportunities in Exporting
- How to Start a Home-based Business

11. Publications on Small Business

US Small Business Administration
PO Box 15434
Fort Worth, TX 67119

The SBA has over 100 business publications, at nominal fees, which address important business topics and answer questions most asked by prospective and existing business owners. Topics include financial management, general management, crime prevention, marketing, personnel management, and new products, ideas, and inventions. A free Directory of Business Development Publications and order forms can be received by contacting your local SBA office or by calling the Small Business Answer Desk.

12. Research and Development

Office of Small Business Innovation Research
National Science Foundation
Room 502, 1800 G Street NW
Washington, DC 20550

This office offers information and guidance on their specific programs and research opportunities for small firms involved in research and technology.

13. Research and Development Funding for Small Business

National Technical Information Service
US Department of Commerce
5285 Port Royal Road
Springfield, VA 22161

The Small Business Guide to Federal Research and Development Funding Opportunities provides contacts to government offices that contract out research and development work. It is written for smaller businesses with strong scientific and technical competence that want to do research and development work with the government. Highlighted is the Small Business Innovation Research (SBIR) Program. This guide gives you steps to obtaining federal R&D funding, an overview of federal laboratory research efforts, criteria companies must meet, and laws and regulations that affect small business. Request information brochure from the above address.

14. Research Studies in Small Business

Office of Economic Research, Office of Advocacy, SBA

The Office of Advocacy coordinates research to promote policies that strengthen the performance of American small business. The *Catalog of Completed Research Studies* is a listing of research studies covering a broad scope of small business topics, including studies on finance and credit, capital formation, taxes and regulation, government competition and procurement, job creation, innovation, women and minority business ownership. Contact the office above to obtain this catalog.

15. Small Business Institutes

SBIs are organized through the SBA on almost 500 colleges and universities around the nation. They are staffed by senior business students and their faculty advisors, and offer free guidance and assistance to small firms. Contact your local SBA district office to obtain the name and telephone number of the SBI nearest you.

16. Financial Management and Your Business

Superintendent of Documents
US Government Printing Office
Washington, DC 20402

Financial Management: How to make a Go of Your Business provides information to familiarize the small business owner with concepts of financial management. Tips on financial planning, cash-flow management, obtaining capital, and other topics are covered.

17. Directories

- *Business Women's Network Directory* provides detailed profiles of the top 400 US business and professional women's organizations. Available from The Business Women's Network, 1146 19th Street NW, Third Floor, Washington, DC 20036.
- *Compendium of National Statistics on Women-Owned Businesses in the US* brings together, in a single document, virtually all the statistical information available on women's business ownership in this country. Included are demographic characteristics of women business owners, and the impact of women's businesses on the economy. The statistics come from the National Foundation for Women Business Owners and from federal agencies. The compendium is available from the National Women's Business Council, 5850-409 Third St. SW, Washington, DC 20024.
- *Complete Eastern/Midwestern/Western States Government Resource Guide.* By Iris Lorenz-Fife. Entrepreneur Inc., 2392 Morse Avenue, PO Box 19787, Irvine, CA. Describes state and federal programs that assist small business in start-up, growth, restructuring or mature phases.
- *Directories in Print.* Annotated guide, issued annually in two volumes, to over 14,000 directories published worldwide. Gale Research Inc., 835 Penobscot Building, Detroit, MI 48226-4094.
- *Encyclopedia of Business Information Sources.* 27-page outline of contents under some 2500 different headings. Gale Research Inc. See above.
- *Free Money for Small Business & Entrepreneurs,* by Laurie Blum, 3rd Edition (John Wiley). This is a comprehensive directory of more than 700 sources of capital for entrepreneurs available from non-profit and government agencies, categorized by region, type of business, where to apply, and how to write proposals.
- *Seminars Directory.* Lists seminars on such topics as computer-assisted instruction, computer-based training, employee orientation, facilitator training, games, interactive instruction, needs analysis, program design and management, tele-training, and training techniques by title and geographic indexes. Gale Research Inc., see above.
- *Trades Shows and Exhibits, Annual Directory of North American Trade and Industrial Shows.* Approximately 500 major headings, 400 sub-headings, under selected major categories. Bill Communications Inc., POB 3078, Southeastern PA 19398-3078
- *Training and Development Organizations Directory.* Covers 2,300 companies, institutes, graduate schools, consulting groups, and other organizations that conduct managerial and supervisory training. Alphabetical arrangement with geographic, subject and personal name indexes. Gale Research, Inc. See above.

18. Group Associations

- *American Association of Black Women Entrepreneurs*, PO Box 13933, Silver Spring, MD 20911-3933
- *American Association of Home Based Business*, PO Box 10023, Rockville, MD 20849
- *Association of Collegiate Entrepreneurs* (ACE) and *Young Entrepreneurs Organization* (YEO). Center for Entrepreneurship, 1845 N. Fairmont, Wichita State Univ., Wichita, KS 67260-0147. ACE members are student entrepreneurs, YEO members are entrepreneurs under the age of 30.
- *Business Women's Network*, a division of the Public Affairs Group, Washington, DC
- *Catalyst House on Women's Issues*, PO Box 70603, Friendship Heights, MD 20813
- *Entrepreneurial Mothers Association*, 375 E. Elliot, Suite 2, Chandle, AZ 85225
- *Environmental Career Opportunities*, PO Box 15629, Chevy Chase, MD 20825
- *Indigenous Women's Network*, c/o Winona LaDuke, White Earth Land Recovery Project, PO Box 327, White Earth, MN 56591
- *Institute for Women's Policy Research (IWPR)*, 1400 - 20th St. NW, Suite 104, Washington, DC 20036
- *International Council for Small Business/US Association for Small Business and Entrepreneurs* (USASBE) 905 University Ave., Room 203, Madison, WI. 53715. Educators and entrepreneurs interested in small business.
- *National Association for the Cottage Industry*, PO Box 14850, Chicago, IL 60614
- *National Association for the Self-Employed* (NASE), PO Box 612067, Dallas, TX 75261. Provides educational programs, group insurance plans, group discounts for travel and business services. It also sponsors charitable and self-help projects through the NASE Foundation.
- *National Association of Female Executives*, Box 469031, Escondido, CA 92046-9925. NAFE offers contacts, opportunities, information, advice, moral support, and its Venture Capital Fund.
- *National Association of Women Business Owners*, 1100 Wayne Avenue, Suite 830, Silver Spring, MD 20910
- *National Business Association*, 5025 Arapaho, Suite 515, Dallas, TX 75248. Provides entrepreneurs with benefits and services in business, lifestyle, health and education. They include student loan assistance, travel discounts, health insurance, a credit union, and a monthly publication, The National Business News.

- *National Federation of Business & Professional Women's Clubs*, 2012 Massachusetts Avenue NW, Washington, DC 20036.
- *National Federation of Independent Business* (NFIB), 53 Century Boulevard, Suite 300, Nashville, TN 37214. Also 600 Maryland Avenue SW, Suite 700, Washington, DC 20024. The country's largest small business association, NFIB, has membership of over 500,000 business owners. Represents small business interests to state and federal governments.
- *National Women's Economic Alliance Foundation*, 1440 New York Avenue, Suite 300, Washington, DC 20005.
- *Non-traditional Employment for Women*, 102 East 22nd Street, Room 710, New York, NY 10010
- *Organization of Chinese American Women*, 1300 N. Street NW, Suite 100, Washington, DC 20005.
- *Renaissance Women*, 205 Third Street SE, Washington, DC 20003.
- *Roundtable for Women in Food Services*, 425 Central Park West, New York, NY 10025.
- *Shorter Work-Time Group*, US, c/o Barbara Brandt, #1 - 69 Dover St., Somerville, MA 02144
- *US Hispanic Chamber of Commerce*, 2000 M Street NW, Suite 860, Washington, DC 20036.
- WISE, *Women's Initiative for Self-Employment*, 450 Mission Street, #460, San Francisco, CA, 94105. A non-profit corporation assisting women in the low to moderate income groups to start or expand their business.
- *Women's Resource Directory (WoRD)*, PO Box 66796, Houston, TX 77266
- *Women Construction Owners & Executives*, USA, PO Box 883034, San Francisco, CA 94188-3034.
- *Women in Government Relations*, Inc., 1325 Massachusetts Avenue NW, Suite 510, Washington, DC 20005-4171.
- *Women to Women Communications* (publisher of international listing of women's magazines), PO Box 161775, Cupertino, CA 95016

19. National Trade Associations

- *American Association of Black Women Entrepreneurs*, PO Box 13933, Silver Springs, MD 20911-3933.
- *American Business Women's Association*, 9100 Ward Parkway, Kansas City, MO 64114.
- *American Society of Women Accountants*, District of Columbia Area Chapter, 11350 Random Hills Road, Suite 800, Fairfax, VA 22030.
- *American Women's Society of Certified Public Accountants*, 401 North Michigan Avenue, Chicago, IL 60611.

- *Black Women's Agenda, Inc.*, 1000 Vermont Avenue NW, Washington, DC 20005.
- *Committee of 200*, 676 North St. Clair, Suite 1900, Chicago, IL 60611.
- *Direct Marketing Association*, 11 West 42nd Street, New York, NY 10038-8096.
- *Federation of Organizations for Professional Women*, 2001 S Street NW, Suite 500, Washington, DC 20009.
- *Financial Women International*, 7910 Woodmont Avenue, Bethesda, MD 20814-3015.
- *National Association for Female Executives*, Inc., 127 West 24th Street, New York, NY 10011.
- *National Association for the Cottage Industries*, PO Box 14850, Chicago, IL 60614.
- *National Association of Black Women Entrepreneurs*, PO Box 1375, Detroit, MI 48231.
- *National Association of Negro Business & Professional Women*, 1806 New Hampshire Avenue NW, Washington, DC 20009.
- *National Association of Women Business Owners* (NAWBO), 600 South Federal Street, Suite 400, Chicago, IL 60605. In California, 900 Wilshire Boulevard, Suite 1434, Los Angeles, CA 90017.

20. Magazines, Newsletters, Internet

Magazines and newsletters are often your most current sources of information. There are thousands of them. This is why librarians are invaluable friends. They can direct you to information on your topic(s) of interest. Then you must do the work, synthesizing data into chunks you can use. So much information is available, your problem is limiting your data collection to truly relevant material and don't forget the vast research resources of the Internet.

You can hire people to do this intensive research for you. University students are often available and generally familiar with data bases and how to find them. Remember, it is your responsibility to be completely informed and current on your topic. That is the least your family, funders, other supporters and yourself, deserve.

21. Smart Sites for Working Women

- **Small Business Administration's Office of Women's Business Ownership Outside Resources Hotlist (www.sbaonline.sba.gov/womeninbusiness/hotlist/)**
  Links to resources for women business owners.
- **Canadian Women's Internet Association (www.women.ca)**
  Government Resource references, job sites, e-mail lists, women in business.
- **Executive Women's Travel Network (www.delta-air.com/womenexecs)**
  Interactive travel forum: tips on safety, packing, fitness and nutrition, and statistics about female business travelers.
- **Smart Business Supersite, The How-To Resource for Business (www.smartbiz.com)**
  Articles, reports, book profiles, business products statistics, and related Internet resources.
- **Today's Parent (www.todaysparent.com)**
  Timely information on parenting, links to other US and Canadian sites.
- **VOWworld — Voices of Women Online (www.voiceofwomen.com)**
  Business opportunities and business services listings.
- **WebSearch, The Business of Women (www.web-search.com/women.html)**
  Database of women-owned businesses with Web sites. Free of charge.
- **Women's Business Resource Site (www.athenet.net/~ccain/)**
  Network, share business venture experiences; link to other business sites, free articles, products and services, and other business resources.
- **Women's Connection Online (www.womenconnect.com)**
  Databases/directories for women in business, particularly entrepreneurs.
- **Women's Wire (women.com)**
  Women's resources and businesses. See *Ask Biz Shrink* to get advice from a marketing firm specializing in women-owned small businesses.
- **Women in Business — Cyberspace Field of Dreams (www.gridley.org/~imaging/links.html)**
  Business support and sales opportunities; bid opportunities for networking women.
- **WWWomen WebRing (www.webring.org)**
  On line tour of women's web sites—A browser's treasure.

APPENDIX II

Sources of Information in Canada

1. Canada Business Service Centres

Federal and provincial governments in Canada have opened excellent *Canada Business Service Centres* (CBSC) in every province.

CBSCs are aimed at new entrepreneurs and established small and medium businesses to give them information they need for making decisions. Designed as "one-stop" centers for business information, each CBSC offers access to almost 900 services and products aimed at local clients.

Now, from provincial phone numbers, you can find out about starting a business, ongoing support for growth and expansion, regulations, financial assistance programs, taxation and trade/export opportunities.

Local CBSCs ensure that national program information is modified for its province and that local contacts are developed for referrals. New information is added and new data is updated frequently. In busier centers, basic information can be obtained by touch-tone phone 24-hours a day; toll-free numbers extend across the country. Information officers are available to direct callers to appropriate people and resources.

Information by Fax

Information can be obtained from each CBSC by requesting a master catalog describing catalogs available. InfoFAX operates 24-hours a day, seven days a week.

To Reach Canada Business Service Centres

British Columbia
Canada/British Columbia Business
Service Centre
601 West Cordova Street
Vancouver, British Columbia
V6B 1G1
Tel: (604)775-5525
Toll Free: (800)667-2272
Fax: (604)775-5520
InfoFAX: (604)775-5515
InfoFAX: (800)667-2272
Internet:
www.sb.gov.bc.ca/smallbus/sbhome.html

Alberta
The Business Link
Business Service Centre
100-10237 104th Street
Edmonton, Alberta
T5J 1B1
Tel: (403)422-7722
Toll Free: 1-800-272-9675
Fax: (403)422-0055
InfoFAX: (403)427-7971
InfoFAX: (800)563-9926
Internet: www.cbsc.org/alberta/

Saskatchewan
Canada/Saskatchewan Business
Service Centre
122 - 3rd Avenue, North
Saskatoon, Saskatchewan
S7K 2H6
Tel: (306)956-2323
Toll Free: (800)667-4374
Fax: (306)956-2328
InfoFAX: (306)956-2310
InfoFAX: (800)667-9433
Internet: www.cbsc.org/sask/

Manitoba
Canada Business Service Centre
330 Portage Avenue, 8th Floor
PO Box 2609
Winnipeg, Manitoba
R3C 4B3
Tel: (204)984-2272
Toll Free: (800)665-2019
Fax: (204)983-3852
InfoFAX: (204)984-5527
InfoFAX: (800)665-9386
Internet: www.cbsc.org/manitoba/

Ontario
Canada - Ontario
Business Call Centre
Toronto, Ontario
M5V 3E5
Tel: (416)954-INFO (4636)
Toll Free: (800)567-2345
Fax: (416)954-8597
Info-FAX: (416)954-8555
Info-FAX: (800)240-4192
Internet: www.cbsc.org/ontario/

Quebec
Info Entrepreneurs
5 Place Ville Marie
Niveau Plaza, Suite 12500, Plaza Level
Montreal, Quebec
H3B 4Y2
Tel: (514)496-INFO (4636)
Toll Free: (800)322-INFOR (4636)
Fax: (514)496-5934
Info-FAX: (514)496-4010
Info-FAX: (800)322-4010
Internet: www.cbsc.org/quebec/

Nova Scotia
Canada/Nova Scotia
Business Service Centre
1575 Brunswick Street
Halifax, Nova Scotia
B3J 2G1
Tel: (902)426-8604
Toll Free: (800)668-1010
Fax: (902)426-6530
Info-FAX: (902)426-3201
Info-FAX: (800)401-3201
TTY: (800)797-4188
Internet: www.cbsc.org/ns/

New Brunswick
Canada/New Brunswick
Business Service Centre
570 Queen Street, PO Box 578
Fredericton, New Brunswick
E3B 6Z6
Tel: (506)444-6140
Toll Free: (800)668-1010
Fax: (506)444-6172
Info-FAX: (506)444-6169
Info-FAX: (800)401-3201
TTY: (800)887-6550
Internet: www.cbsc.org/nb/

Prince Edward Island
Canada/Prince Edward Island
Business Service Centre
75 Fitzroy Street
PO Box 40
Charlottetown, PEI
C1A 7K2
Tel: (902)368-0771
Toll Free: (800)668-1010
Fax: (902)566-7377
Info-FAX: (902)368-0776
Info-FAX: (800)401-3201
TTY: (020)368-0724
Internet: www.cbsc.org/pei/

Newfoundland
Canada Business Service Centre
90 O'Leary Avenue
PO Box 8687
St. John's, Newfoundland
A1B 3T1
Tel: (709)772-6022
Toll Free: (800)668-1010
Fax: (709)772-6090
Info-FAX: (709)772-6030
Internet: www.cbsc.org/nfld/

Northwest Territories
Canada/NWT
Business Service Centre
3rd Floor, Northern United Place
5004 - 54th Street
Yellowknife, NWT
X1A 2L9
Tel: (403)873-7958
Toll Free: (800)661-0599
Fax: (403)873-0101
Info-FAX: (403)873-0575
Info-FAX: (800)661-0825
Internet: www.cbsc.org/nwt/

Yukon
Canada/Yukon
Business Service Centre
201-208 Main Street
Whitehorse, Yukon
Y1A 2A9
Tel: (403)633-6257
Toll Free: (800)661-0543

2. Statistics Canada

"StatsCan" is Canada's national statistical agency; it has a mandate to collect information on the activities and social condition of Canadians. The Agency maintains hundreds of data bases containing reliable information about Canada, its economy and its people. There is an extraordinary amount of information available. Your best bet is to telephone the local regional office and enjoy their cheerful service.

3. Canadian Women's Groups

Canadian women can find professional support and networking advantages from business women's groups. Here are a few:

- Canadian Association of Women Executives and Entrepreneurs, Toronto, Ontario (416)482-2933
- Canadian Federation of Business & Professional Women's Clubs Ottawa, Ontario (613)234-7619. With 77 clubs in Canada, call to find out which is closest to you.
- The Woman Inventors Project, Toronto, Ontario, (905)731-0328
- Women's Entrepreneurship Program, Toronto, Ontario, (416)978-3831. Offers courses, conferences and workshops, along with the Canadian Woman Entrepreneur of the Year awards. (Awards info: (905)472-0774).
- Women Entrepreneurs of Canada (WEC). The Official Canadian Chapter of a world-wide organization, Les Femmes chef d'Enterprises Mondiales (FCEM), a resource for women who have successfully launched their businesses. Toronto, Ontario (416)866-1125
- Women's Enterprise Bureau, Newfoundland, (709)754-5555
- Women's Business Association, Vancouver, BC (604)688-0951
- Alberta Women's Enterprise Initiative Association, Calgary and Edmonton (800)713-3558
- Canadian Federation of Independent Business, Toronto, Ontario (416)534-7324
- Canadian Women's Foundation; Women and Economic Development Consortium, Toronto, Ontario (416)365-1745
- Shorter Work-Time Network, Canada, Courtenay, BC (250)334-0998

4. The Business Development Bank of Canada

The Business Development Bank of Canada (BDC) is a Crown corporation whose mission is to help create and develop Canadian small and medium-sized businesses.

The BDC provides specialized financing for viable business projects as well as a wide range of business counseling, training and mentoring services. BDC is the only national financial institution to offer this unique one-stop-shopping approach for helping Canadian entrepreneurs. With both financial and management services under one roof, the bank is able to provide entrepreneurs with complete solutions to their business needs.

BDC's business training and mentoring programs, Step-Up and Step-In, are designed especially for women. They also hold workshops and conferences for women and produce a booklet entitled *Financing a Small Business: A Guide for Women Entrepreneurs*, as well as a study called *Women in Business — A Collective Profile.*

BDC's services are made available across Canada through a broad network of 78 branches. For more information, contact the branch nearest you.

5. Federal Government Small Business Loans Act

Under the Federal Government's Small Business Loans Act, an entrepreneur can borrow up to $250,000 to finance new equipment or real estate, or to renovate facilities (subject to qualifications of SBLA which include revenues not exceeding $5 million per year).

Up to 90% financing is available at fixed or floating interest rates. Repayment terms may be up to 10 years depending on the life of the asset. The application fee of two percent of the loan amount, payable to the Federal Government, can be included in the principal amount (subject to $250,000 maximum) and financed over the life of the loan.

To obtain information, inquire at the provincial Canada Business Service Centers.

6. Status of Women Canada

Status of Women Canada (SWC) is the Federal Government agency responsible for policy, research, funding and technical assistance, and communications for the promotion of women's equality in Canada. SWC provides assistance through regional representatives, regular contact with women's groups across the country, and a formal consultation function to promote sharing of information and resources.

SWC produces regular and special publications, manages media services and provides library assistance. Human resources, financial and material management, information technology, security and telecommunications activities are also provided. Contact:

Status of Women Canada
700 - 360 Albert Street
Ottawa, Ontario K1A 1C3

7. Western Economic Diversification Canada

> Funded by WD, the various provincial organizations noted here are lenders of last resort in Western Canada. They support at the start-up stage, women intending to become self-employed, or who are looking to expand existing businesses.

Western Economic Diversification (WD) is a federal, but community-driven initiative designed to enhance the range of services and capital available to women entrepreneurs in Western Canada. WD is particularly aimed at small and medium-sized enterprises developing new products, new markets, new technology and import replacements.

It was established in 1994 following research which found that women entrepreneurs need improved access to financing, training, information, mentoring, counseling and networking.

By working with community organizations, youth groups, educators, and other grassroots advisors, WD will help promote entrepreneurship as a career option to women. WD is located in Western Canada at addresses noted below:

- Women's Enterprise Society of British Columbia
  7 - 20070 Harvey Ave.
  Kelowna, BC V1Y 8P8
- Alberta Women's Enterprise Initiative Association
  100 - 10237 104 Street NW
  Edmonton, Alberta T5J 1B1
- Women Entrepreneurs of Saskatchewan Inc.
  112 - 2100 8th Street East
  Saskatoon, Saskatchewan S7H 0V1
- Manitoba Women's Enterprise Centre Inc.
  130 - 240 Graham Avenue
  Winnipeg, Manitoba R3C 0J7

8. The Canadian Embassy, Washington, DC

Judith Bradt, Director of Government Markets for the Canadian Embassy in Washington, DC, invites your inquiry about exporting to the United States. There is a free, highly sophisticated service available to help you investigate contacts, market opportunities, financing and all necessary procedures for doing business in a market 12 times the size of Canada's. Free Trade and NAFTA have opened exciting opportunities for doing business in the US—as some 23,000 Canadian firms are already doing. Contact:

Judith A. Bradt
Director of Government Markets
The Canadian Embassy
501 Pennsylvania Avenue NW
Washington, DC 20001
Internet: judith.bradt@wshdc01.x400.gc.ca

APPENDIX III

Questions — A Workbook of Questions

Key Personal Questions, (chapter 2, page 17)

	Yes	No
1. Do you understand yourself and your potential, that which makes you enthusiastic about undertaking something?	❑	❑
2. When you believe in something, can you convince others of its merits?	❑	❑
3. Success depends on desire, will-power, and personal discipline. Do you have these?	❑	❑
4. Although you consider other people's opinions, do you keep the right to make final decisions?	❑	❑
5. Do you believe that steps to success include setting personal goals and planning how to achieve them?	❑	❑
6. Do you enjoy giving your best to everything you do, and does successful completion give you a feeling of satisfaction?	❑	❑
7. Do you want to be your own boss, making your own decisions, although it will require work and discipline?	❑	❑
8. Do you feel comfortable managing other people, making decisions which affect them?	❑	❑
9. Do you believe you can motivate staff, colleagues, business partners and employees?	❑	❑
10. Will you work hard, long hours, and do several things at once?	❑	❑
11. When you decide to do something, do you give it your all, and complete it?	❑	❑
12. Do you find unexpected situations stimulating?	❑	❑
13. Do you agree that money is a good measure of success, but not the only one?	❑	❑

	Yes	No
14. Do you agree that the trick of life is to learn how to solve problems and adjust to changes?	❑	❑
15. Do you agree that success is not the result of luck, but of good planning and hard work (maybe fertilized with luck!)?	❑	❑
16. Do you check on the results of your decisions, and reflect whether or not they were good decisions, and what you've learned since?	❑	❑
17. Are you often thinking of new and better ways to do things?	❑	❑
18. Do you find it hard to do nothing? Does the sense of accomplishment that goes with getting things done give you energy?	❑	❑
19. Can you make long-term commitments and plans to get where you want to go?	❑	❑
20. Are your parents, relatives or close friends now, or previously in business?	❑	❑
21. Do you have previous experience managing individuals and work?	❑	❑
22. Do you enjoy participating in clubs, associations and groups, and having different responsibilities?	❑	❑
23. In your spare time, do you like to research practical, concrete ideas?	❑	❑
24. Do you have energy for concentrated effort and long hours?	❑	❑
25. Do you have the self-direction to work alone?	❑	❑
26. Do you have techniques to control stress?	❑	❑
27. Do you have the confidence to accept failures and turn them into opportunities?	❑	❑
28. Can you communicate feelings and dreams to family?	❑	❑
29. Will you keep your family informed and involved?	❑	❑
30. Will you be able to say "no" to leisure activities if necessary? Will those who go without you understand?	❑	❑

	Yes	No
31. Will you be able to maintain a personal and family life as well as run a business?	☐	☐
32. Can you prepare yourself to not have a personal life for some time?	☐	☐
33. Will you be able to budget business expenses and stick to the limits you set?	☐	☐
34. Do you understand financial statements and why they are important to a business?	☐	☐
35. Do you appreciate the importance of tracking expenses, inventory and debt?	☐	☐
36. Are alternate sources of income available for living expenses?	☐	☐
37. Are you realistic about expenses and sources of income until the business gets established?	☐	☐
38. Is your home-life financially organized and can business income and expenses be kept separate from household demand?	☐	☐
39. Does every family member appreciate your goals and how important the business is to you? Do they support you?	☐	☐
40. Will your home life remain stable if the business fails?	☐	☐
41. Are you realistic about how long success may take and committed to making the business work?	☐	☐
42. Are your planning skills and sense of responsibility strong enough to build a successful venture?	☐	☐
43. Do you have the knowledge to make this particular business succeed, or should you be securing that knowledge before going into business?	☐	☐
44. Do you want business success enough to set and keep high standards of product and service?	☐	☐

The answers to almost all of these questions should be "yes," but there is no right or wrong yes/no totals. You will see the picture.

Choosing Advisors (chapter 3, page 21)

The importance of choosing advisors VERY carefully cannot be over-emphasized… and there is one huge trap to avoid. Choose advisors for their professional competence and experience, not just because it's "good ol' Uncle Charlie." Sometimes having objectivity is difficult, particularly if Uncle Charlie is saying "go for it" and offering to "…help you all I can."

My advice would be to start the search through your banker who is usually pretty objective, and should be of assistance in helping you to assess and select key professional advisors. In doing so, your banker will reveal to you his real interest and commitment towards helping you.

1. Was the professional recommended by someone you know? Why?
2. Did you know in advance whether you would be billed for the consultation?
3. Is small business their specialty?
4. Does their practice include other clients with your kind of business?
5. Were your questions answered clearly, in language you understood?
6. Did they make recommendations as to what you should do next?
7. Did fees quoted seem reasonable?
8. Were they obviously interested in having your account?
9. Are you comfortable with this professional?
10. Do you want this person on your team?

(By the way, don't ever be intimidated by a common image of "bankers"— That they are sort of superhuman. They are not. They are business people, renting money, and they should compete to be able to rent some to you!)

Start Your Financial Planning (chapter 3 page 24)

Being able to answer these questions will give you a great boost in confidence. You will sound professional about your business plan.

1. How long will it be before the business generates an income?
2. Do you know your financial needs to start, and to cover expenses until income commences?
3. How much can you raise yourself?
4. How much will you need to borrow?
5. Have you allowed for the following:
   - Rent
   - Utilities
   - Telephone
   - Equipment
   - Supplies
   - Advertising/Promotion
   - Wages/Salaries
   - Licenses/Patents
   - Professional Fees
   - Insurance
   - Taxes
   - Miscellaneous
6. Have you allowed for a reasonable income for yourself?
7. Have you estimated the capital needed for your first year?
8. Have you consulted with your accountant on sources of start-up capital for your first year?
9. Have you completed a projected balance sheet, income statement and cash flow chart for your first three years?

Generating Ideas (chapter 5, page 35)
Types of Opportunities to Explore

Here are some broad ideas to start you thinking:

- Cater to Niche Markets
- Add Value to Existing Products
- Find Uses for Waste Materials
- Combine Components
- Find People with Under-used Skills
- Take Advantage of a Market Shift
- Cover Market Gaps or Shortages
- Improve an Existing Idea
- Imitate a Successful Idea
- Find a Good Product That Has Failed
- Transfer a Concept from One Industry to Another
- Invent a New Product or Service
- Locate a Patent Opportunity
- Market Someone Else's Product
- Become an Agent
- Become a Distributor
- Become an Import Distributor or Agent
- Become an Export Distributor
- Serve Unique Client Groups
- Offer Discount Goods for Resale
- Plan and Promote Events
- Create a Market Demand
- Identify Opportunities From Your Current Business
- Identify the Full Scope of Your Business
- Provide a Consultation or Information Service
- Buy an Existing Business or Franchise
- Manufacture and Market Under License
- Assemble a Product
- Recycle an Existing Product
- Become a Supplier
- Replace Imports

Questions you should ask, and answer, about any business idea you are considering (chapter 5, page 37)

1. **Introduction**

   Write a simple description of your business idea. What do you want to do? Why? Where do you want to do it? What is the product or service you want to provide? Who will buy it? How will buyers use it? Do you have a target niche? Have you a competitive advantage for that niche?

2. **Personal Considerations**
   - Is this idea something you can really get excited about?
   - Would you sacrifice lifestyle to turn this idea into a successful business?
   - Is the idea legal and ethical?
   - Do you want to work with the people associated with this idea?
   - Do you want to live the lifestyle required by this idea?
   - Does the work match activities you like?
   - Do you have the health and energy to operate this business?
   - Does your personality suit this business?
   - What knowledge, skills or experience do you have to carry out this idea?
   - Do you have knowledge of this industry, information on competitors, potential clients, markets and current technology?
   - Do you have adequate managerial skills to operate this business? If not, can you learn them or employ someone with those skills?
   - Could you handle failure, losing assets, damaging your ego?
   - Do you have enough money?

3. **Market Considerations**
   - What is your target market? Where are they? What are their demographics, e.g. age, income, marital status, number of children, type of housing, etc. How many are there?
   - Have you surveyed potential customers for their opinions of your planned prices, packaging, promotion and distribution strategies?
   - What patterns of buying behavior are important for this product or service? i.e.:
     - When do people buy?
     - How do they buy similar products or services?
     - What is the typical size of orders?
     - Who makes the decision to buy?
     - How much effort is needed to persuade the buyer?

- How many orders or contracts can you have in hand before starting the business?
  - Where will you find your first orders?
  - What does an analysis of the competition illustrate?
    Market Shares? Strategies? Profitability?
  - If a client does not buy your product or service, whose do they purchase?
  - Who are the main suppliers of those alternate products?
  - What are market trends regarding those alternate products?
- Sales will probably be at the expense of competitors. How will they react?
- What competitive advantage does your idea have over those of your competition?
- How will you protect yourself from the competition?
  Can you have a lower price? A higher price?
  Lower quality? Higher quality?
- Can others quickly copy your idea?
- How much of a head start do you have over competitors for this idea?
- Who will sell your product or service?
  For how much?
  What sales tools will they need?
  What training will they need?
- How will your product or service be promoted?
  What forms of advertising will be used?
  Can you handle promotion and advertising yourself or will you hire someone to do it?
  How much money will you spend on promotion and advertising?
  How much money is the competition spending and where?
- What does a detailed analysis of distribution illustrate?
  How will you distribute your products?
  How much inventory will you need?
  Is one product line enough?
  Is there enough repeat business involved?
  Note: Distribution of product is one of the major hurdles to consider. Begin a dialogue with distributors. Ask retailers for their recommendations on which distributors to approach.

4. Product Considerations

- Can you produce or deliver the service?
- How have you assured yourself that the product or service will really work?
- Can you find facilities to use?

- How much development work is needed before units can be produced or the service delivered?
- What legalities need to be checked (patents, zoning laws, etc.)?
- How many units can you produce or how many customers can you serve in the first year?
- Can you find materials at a reasonable price?
- Can you find good production staff?
- What equipment will be needed?
  - Where can the equipment be bought or rented?
  - What servicing and maintenance will the equipment require?
  - What are the delivery times for equipment and materials?
- Can you assemble a management team to develop the opportunity?
  - What management and technical skills are needed? Are they available?
  - Does this group have the personal contacts that will be needed?

5. Financial Considerations

- What revenue can you achieve from sales? To determine this, multiply the actual prices you will receive for products or services by the estimated number of sales, based on the interest expressed by potential customers.
- Are your prices in line with the competition? If not, why not?
- How will customers react to the price, based on their perception of your quality of the product or service? Ask your potential retailers and/or distributors.
- Are your margins in line with industry standards? If not, why not? How will customers react to the margins they earn with your product? Is the margin sufficient to generate the required gross profit, given the volume projections? What margin does the distributor require?
- What will the cost of goods be for the products you produce and/or distribute?
- How will the gross profit compare with other firms in the industry?
- What will the start-up costs be for your business? Consider fixtures, equipment, inventory, legal fees, licenses, advertising, promotion, staff recruitment, etc.
- What will the operating costs be for the business? Consider salaries, rent supplies, interest, office expenses, etc.
- How will the net profit level compare with those of other firms in the industry? What are the causes of higher (or lower) profit levels?
- Can you obtain the money required for this idea?
  - Where will this money come from and on what terms?
  - What collateral can you pledge to secure the loan?

  - How will the loan be repaid if the business fails?
  - What credit can be obtained for materials and supplies?
- Can you survive financially during the early phases of the business? How much money will you need to draw for personal expenses? Include this amount in your cash flow projections.
- Is the level of financial risk low, average or high?
- How much money will be lost if the business fails?
- How can the idea be tested with little or no investment up front?

Are You Alert To Trends? (chapter 6, page 39)

This is a brief guide to the 16 Trends in Faith Popcorn's book *Clicking*.[1] These trends will germinate many new entrepreneurial businesses.

- **Cocooning** — The stay-at-home Trend, reflecting our strong desire to build soft and cozy nests in order to protect ourselves from the harsh, unpredictable realities of the outside world.
- **Clanning** — The inclination to join up, belong to, hang out with groups of like kinds, providing a secure feeling that our own belief systems will somehow be validated by consensus.
- **Fantasy Adventure** — As a break from modern tensions, we actively seek excitement in basically risk-free adventures, whether it be via travel, food, or Virtual Reality.
- **Pleasure Revenge** — Consumers tired of all the rules and regulations, want to cut loose and have secret bacchanals with a bevy of forbidden fruits.
- **Small Indulgences** — Stressed-out from ever-increasing expenses, consumers are finding ways to reward themselves with affordable luxuries.
- **Anchoring** — A new Trend that tracks the recent phenomenon of reaching back to our spiritual roots, taking what was comforting from the past in order to be securely anchored in the future.
- **Egonomics** — In a direct reaction to the sterile computer era, we are looking for new ways to make more personal statements. Thus, businesses that market to the "I" and provide exceptional service should excel.
- **Female Think** — A Trend that reflects a new set of business and societal values, encouraging us to shift marketing consciousness from the traditional goal-oriented, hierarchical models to the more caring and sharing, familial ones.

---

[1] *Clicking*, Faith Popcorn, Harper Collins, 1996.

- **Mancipation** — A NewThink for men that goes beyond being "strictly business" and warmly embraces the freedom of being an individual.
- **99 Lives** — A new look at the modern motto of "Too Fast a Pace, Too Little Time," which forces us all to assume multiple roles in order to cope with busy, high-tech lives.
- **Cashing Out** — Working women and men, questioning the intrinsic value of a high-powered career, are opting for more fulfillment from a simpler way of living.
- **Being Alive** — There's a growing awareness that a new concept of "wellness" can add generous years of good health, giving us an overall better quality to our lives.
- **Down-Aging** — Nostalgia for a carefree childhood lets us introduce a new sense of lightness into our often-too-serious adult lives.
- **Vigilante Consumer** — A scanning of the various ways the frustrated, often angry consumer can manipulate the marketplace through pressure, protest, and politics.
- **Icon Toppling** — A new socioquake has transformed mainstream America and the world, forcing us to question and often reject our monuments of business/government, the long-accepted "pillars of society."
- **S.O.S. (Save Our Society)** — In order to protect our endangered planet, we must rediscover a social conscience based on a necessary blend of ethics, passion and compassion.

About Franchises (chapter 6, page 42)

1. Questions to ask a franchisee:

- How long have you owned your franchise? Have you more than one?
- Will you renew your contract?
- Will you buy more outlets? If not, why not?
- Is this a full-time job? What are the hours like?
- Do you really love it? Would you buy it again?
- Has the business turned out as you expected?
  Was the franchisor realistic?
- What background/skills are needed to succeed in this business?
- Have you received all training and support promised?
  Was it as expected?
- How much did you make last year in personal income?
- What's the potential?
- Do you know of any reason not to buy this franchise?

2. Then ask the franchisor:

- For details on training programs and ongoing support:
  How much focus is on these areas?
- How is a franchisee territory protected from competing franchisees or company stores?
- What background does the franchisor seek in a franchisee?
- How quickly has the company grown in recent years?
- What has the company got planned for the future?
- How does the company management differ from that of competitors?

3. Then ask yourself:

- Could you love this business?
- Would you bounce out of bed early on a wet, dark, cold, foggy morning, raring to get to work?
- Would you be losing sight of what you really want, when getting the strong sell from a franchisor?
- Has the part-time home business you envisioned turned into an operation requiring 70-hour weeks, including nights and weekends?
- Would you go over your original financial plan for starting a business?
- Have you **really** looked at the fine print in the contracts involved?
- Have you made the smart investment of getting strong professional financial and legal advice, for this large decision?
- If this is a fairly new franchise, are you moving **extra** cautiously?

Is Working at Home for You? (chapter 7, page 45)

- Does the concept of working from home please you?
- Do you enjoy working alone, or without a lot of people around you?
- Do you like your home, and being in it, working in any outfits you choose, returning to your desk at odd hours, having easy access to an outdoor stretch?
- Are you self-disciplined? Would you know what to do each day and do it?
- Do you like the idea of not having a "boss"?
- Are you good at "prioritizing" tasks?
- Can you resist distractions?
- Are you "now-is-the time" oriented? Is this the right time in your life to be home-based, perhaps because it's better for parenting or because you find commuting strenuous?
- Have you accumulated enough capital to strike out on your own. Are you getting older and don't want to be in the marketplace any longer?

You may feel that some of these questions just need quick "yes, of course" answers. You know that's too easy, and it is only yourself you are fooling. For instance, most everyone would like not to have a boss, right? Now consider the uncomfortable decisions, actions, responsibilities borne by bosses you have known. Have you ever said, "glad it's the boss' problem, not mine"? Well, now those problems will be yours. Do you want them?

Sharing Quotient Quiz (chapter 7, page 47)

Use this quiz to give you and your partner a good hard look at how you're currently dividing responsibilities. If you find that things don't add up as equally as you'd like, change some of the household responsibilities.

Who is doing the:

- laundry
- cooking
- repairs and maintenance, (house, yard, car)
- finances
- daily cleaning, dishes
- heavy duty cleaning
- grocery shopping
- pet care
- childcare, i.e. dressing, bathing, homework, recreation, extracurricular activities

Home-Based Business Opportunities (chapter 7 page 48)

This list just touches on the incredible range of business ventures being carried out from home-based quarters. Some ideas for home-based businesses:

- Animal boarding, care
- Answering service
- Art Gallery and sales
- Audio and visuals production service
- Baby items
- Baking, specialty products
- Bed and Breakfast
- Building Inspection
- Beekeeping, honey production
- Child Care, elderly care, special needs support
- Car services, specialized
- Catering, food or sector specialty
- Children and specialty entertainment, e.g. clowns, magicians
- Cleaning, house commercial/ institutional
- Consultant, wide range of services and subjects
- Convention and conference planning, logistics and support
- Cooking services, specialty or targeted
- Design and layout, creative services in producing documents and audio-visuals
- Distributing
- Door-to-door selling
- Energy services, energy loss, detection, energy efficient planning and renovation
- Event and party planning
- Farming, specialty, including organic, herb, special product (kiwi, holly)
- Fashions, specialty (maternity, children's clothing, appliqué)
- Food products, particularly those tied to trends, natural food, non-beef items, low fat, concern with food purity and quality
- Footwear
- Fundraising
- Furniture polishing, wax, stain
- Furniture repair, small-scale manufacture
- Gardening, yard and lawn maintenance, landscaping
- Gift basket service
- Glass blowing and design, retail and industrial/commercial
- Guided tours and sight-seeing
- Hobby, craft and art supplies

- Home renovations and maintenance
- Image consulting, wardrobe, communication, and executive seminars for professionals
- Importing
- Information service, consulting or information processing
- Interior design, commercial or residential
- Jewelry, original designs and work, repair
- Leisure activities, providing instruction
- Mail order service
- Maternity fashions and specialty products
- Media productions and services
- Microcomputer services: Convert files from one machine format to another.
- Design, create, do layout, publish.
- Manage other people's data.
- Provide mail order services.
- Publish price lists, catalogs, listings, newsletters.
- Rent equipment or time on a computer system.
- Write or print résumés, prospectuses, proposals, reports.
- Sell data.
- Teach about computing or using available software programs, teach other skills and subjects.
- Troubleshoot, problem solve.
- Write programs
- Novelty items (T-shirts, mugs) targeted to certain market, e.g. new parents or grandparents
- Office planning, office systems design, installation
- Packaging, retail and "breaking bulk," sorting large quantities into smaller ones and repackaging them for sale
- Personal services, house sitting, errands
- Personal shopping
- Photo postcards
- Picture postcards
- Photography and photographic services
- Polishes and cleaning products
- Placement and assistance (temporary help) services
- Pool cleaning
- Pottery, particularly specialty styles and products
- Printshop, various services related to copying, printing, document production
- Professions that don't require special facilities, e.g. accountant, lawyer, public relations and management consultants

- Property Management
- Publishing and publishing services (editing)
- Rebuilding or remanufacturing
- Recreation
- Research
- Résumés
- Seminars and courses, workshops
- Services to business—accounting, advertising, temporary help, training etc.
- Sewing and tailoring
- Shoe repair
- Sports equipment
- Telephone soliciting service
- Training and training materials
- Tutoring and instruction
- Videotaping
- Word Processing
- Writing

Is a Home-Base Realistic for You? (chapter 7, page 50)

Use these questions and the *Sharing Quotient Quiz* below to assess whether starting a home-based business is realistic for you:

- **Legalities** — Is your home-based business legal according to zoning by-laws? What restrictions may limit you?
- **Physical Space** — Do you have enough space? Will you have to re-model? At what cost? What effects will a changed use of space have on your family?
- **Family** — Do you have the support of family members? Will the family actively help you and support you… or just leave you alone? Do you know what your family truly thinks about your idea, emotionally as well as logically?
- **Neighborhood** — How might your business affect relationships between your household and your neighbors?
- **Work Style** — Are you a self-starter, disciplined about working on your own? What social or professional activities could replace action you'll miss from an outside place of work?
- **Balance** — Can you be disciplined about maintaining a balance between home life and working at home, between your business and your personal life, between your own growth and that of your business?

Checklist for Starting Your Own Home-Based Business (chapter 7, page 50)

1. **Business Concept**
   - What type of business will you start?
   - Is there a need and can you fill it?
   - Do you have a good understanding of how to market your business?
   - Which business structure have you chosen and why?
   - Are all agreements in place?
   - Is your business name registered?
   - Have you obtained professional advice: legal, tax, accounting, insurance, etc.

2. **The Marketing Strategy**
   - What is your customer profile?
   - What is the market or trading area of your business?
   - Estimate total sales volumes for your business.
   - What will motivate prospective customers to buy?

- What benefits do your products or services offer compared to the competition?
- What is your pricing policy?
- What selling and promotion methods do competitors use?
- How will you distribute products or deliver services?
- What selling techniques have you chosen?
- What promotion methods will you use?

3. Operations and Administration
- If home-based, what changes are needed for office/shop space?
- Will your home work space be large enough, separate, quiet, well lit?
- Is your home work space organized: telephone, work area, equipment, production processes?
- Are business/professional activities and personal/household activities physically separated?
- Is professional advice being obtained on a regular basis: legal, accounting, bookkeeping, industry expert, business advisor, other?
- Have you planned your insurance needs and secured adequate coverage?
- Are furniture, equipment, and machinery needs itemized?
- Can used, recycled or leased items reduce equipment costs?
- Are plans for hiring, training and paying employees in place?
- Are you going to sub-contract work instead of having employees, in order to simplify paper work and maintain business flexibility?
- Are business needs for supplies and materials itemized and incorporated into financial projections?
- How will you handle expansion, unexpected success or high demand?
- How will you handle unexpectedly low sales, sagging markets, unanticipated fewer sales than you projected?

4. Laws and Regulations
- Have the required licenses and permits been obtained?
- Is the business in compliance with all zoning, and municipal bylaws?
- Are all levels of taxes covered in your financial plans?

5. Financing and Cost Control
- Have you determined start-up costs?
- What are your sales forecasts, expenses and profits?
- What is your break-even sales level?
- Have you prepared one realistic and one pessimistic forecast for each key financial area?
- How will you control costs and expenses?

- How much working or operating capital will you need?
- Are funds available for unforeseen start-up difficulties?
- How much of your own money will you be able to invest?
- Where can you borrow or obtain additional funds?
- Have you discussed financing with lending institutions?
- Have you prepared a list of personal and business assets that may be needed for security/collateral?
- Has a separate bank account been opened for the business?
- Have bookkeeping and filing systems been put in place?

6. You, the Business Owner/Operator

- Is your business plan completed?
- Are you confident managing many responsibilities at the same time?
- Are your expectations about yourself as an entrepreneur realistic?
- Do you have management skills or are you taking steps to develop them?
- Most important of all—Is your business going to be something you love to do?

Assessing your product or service is a much bigger task than it might seem here. To evaluate many of the above questions will take time and research. The answers will form a large part of your business plan.

Preparing Your Business Plan (chapter 8, page 51)

1. Have you decided the legal form for business and why?
2. Have you chosen a name?
3. Are you able to complete legal, registration, licensing and insurance requirements?
4. Can you state the primary objective of your business in simple terms?
5. Have you determined if employees will be needed, and what skills they require?
6. Can you describe your product/service in detail, including costs to produce it, final costs to consumers, why your product/service is better than your competition, your suppliers; your customers, potential for future growth?
7. Can you provide details of your personal financial commitment, and where it comes from?
8. Can you provide details of any other funding?
9. Can you itemize additional financial requirements not covered by existing financing?

Meet Your Lender (chapter 8 page 53)

Before any lender can give advice on your proposal, the lender will want to know a great deal about you. Such things as:

1. Do you know what kind of loan you are looking for and why?
2. Can you state why you want to go into business for yourself?
3. Do you have relevant work experience?
4. Do you have degrees or diplomas?
5. Have you taken courses or special training?
6. Do you have special talents or skills to help you?
7. Do you have advisors to supply skills you lack?
8. Do you have a good personal credit rating?
9. Do you have personal assets such as cash savings, stocks and/or bonds, real estate, automobile etc.
10. Do you know your personal net worth?
11. Are your personal assets greater than your personal liabilities (e.g. mortgages, credit card debts, car loans, etc?

Business Plan Format (chapter 10, page 74)

Very early in your discussions with a financial institution ask if they have business plan formats that they like to see used in applications to them. If they do, ask for several copies, to allow for rough drafts. Follow their instructions to the letter, mimic their examples, conform to text lengths and detail required. Better still, see if your potential lender has got small business plan software—It's often supplied free!

A. Executive Summary

- Company name, address and phone number
- Contact person, name and phone number
- Paragraph nature of company business and market area
- Company mission statement
- Security offered to investors
- Business loans sought
- Highlights of Business Plan—preferably one page maximum
- Pay great attention to this page so that reader will retain interest and continue reading.
- Table of Contents
- Section titles and page numbers

B. Part I — Business Concept

1. Description of the Industry

- Industry outlook and potential
- Markets and customers
- Competitive companies
- National and economic trends

2. Description of Business Venture

- Product(s) or service(s)
- Product protection/exclusive rights
- Overall industry target market
- Competitive advantage of your business concept
- Business location and size (location(s)
- Staff and equipment needed
- Brief history

3. Business Goals

- One year specific goals, such as gross sales, profit margins, share of market, opening new store, new product, etc.
- Three-year (as in one year, but not as much detail)
- Over the longer term return on investment, business net worth, sale of business

4. Marketing Plan

- Company market target
- Sales strategy
- Distribution
- Pricing
- Promotion— media, promotions, publicity
- Guarantees—product guarantees and service warranties
- Research

5. Sales Forecast

- One never has all the necessary information, so state the assumptions made in developing the forecast
- Monthly forecast for coming year
- Annual forecast for following 2-4 years
- Note: The sales forecast is the starting point for your projected income statement and cash flow forecast in Part II.

6. Production Plan (Manufacturing)

- Brief description of production process
- Physical plant requirements
- Machinery and equipment
- Raw materials
- Inventory requirements
- Suppliers
- Personnel required
- Cost of facilities, equipment and materials
- Capital estimates

7. Production Plan (Retail or Service)

- Purchasing plans
- Inventory system
- Space requirements
- Staff and equipment required

8. Corporate Structure

- Legal form—proprietorship, partnership, corporation
- Share distribution
- Contracts and agreements—management, shareholder or partnership agreement, franchisor agreement, service contract
- Directors and officers
- Background of key management personnel
- Contract professionals/consultants
- Organization Chart
- Duties and responsibilities of key personnel

9. Risk Assessment

- Critical external factors—strikes, recession, new technology, weather, competition, supplier, consumer demand, etc.
- Critical internal factors—sales off, sales double, key manager quits, workers unionize, etc.
- Contingency plan to handle most significant internal and external risks

10. Action Plan

- Flow charts to accomplish this year's goals—action to be taken and by whom
- Checkpoints for measuring results—identify significant dates, sales and production levels, as decision points

11. Operating Loan

- Line of credit applied for
- Maximum operating cash requirement—cash flow forecast

12. Present Financing

- Term loans outstanding—balance, terms, purpose, security held
- Current operating line of credit

13. References

- Name of present lending institution
- Address and phone number of your Lawyer and Accountant, other key individuals

14. Appendix

- The following documents may be requested by your lender:
- Personal net worth statement to substantiate the value of your personal guarantee if it is required for security
- Letters of intent—potential orders, customer commitments, letters of support
- Proposed list of inventory
- Proposed list of leasehold improvements
- Proposed list of fixed assets—serial numbers
- Cost estimates

C. Part II — Financial Plan

1. Financial Forecasts

- Opening balance sheet
- Projected income statements for next year; for following two years. Use sales forecast as starting point)
- Cash Flow forecast

2. Financing and Capitalization

- Term loan applied for
- Purpose of term loan
- Owner's equity
- Summary of term loan requirements
- Position of an investor—share participation, role in company, etc.
- Description of proposed insurance coverage
- Copies of legal agreements—contracts, lease, franchise agreement, mortgage, debenture
- Appraisals—property, equipment

- Financial statements for associated companies
- Credit terms given and expected

3. Final Preparatory Step

- Follow a format approved by your potential lender. Preparing a business plan will generate a lot of thought and a lot of paper! The final document is a summary of your planning process. Always keep your working papers to substantiate a particular point.
- Have key employees and two or three Board members review the finished plan. There may be something you overlooked or underemphasized. A critical review is good preparation for your presentation to potential investors and lenders.

4. Approaching Lenders

- When approaching any financial institution, you are selling the merits of your business proposal. As in all sales, consider the needs of the other party:
- Your ability to service the debt, repay in full
- Your track record/integrity, personal credit history
- Your level of commitment—equity in the business or cash investment in the asset being purchased
- Secondary source of repayment—security in the event of default; other sources of income. Discuss this with your lawyer
- Lead time—a lender needs a reasonable time to assess your proposal. Don't overdo it—be sensible with the amount of initial documentation

5. Attracting Investors

- First, approach people you know, i.e. friends, bank, credit union or trust company manager, lawyer, accountant, doctor. They may know of other possible investors. If your business concept exhibits high growth potential, a second alternative is to approach a venture capital company. Either way, take a moment to consider the investor's needs, which may differ from a lender's needs:
- Your level of commitment, sharing of risks
- Share participation
- Rate of Return—investors will take a high risk but expect a high rate of return
- Involvement in key decisions, possibly as a director or officer
- Regular financial reporting

D. Part III — Preparing A Cash Flow Forecast (chapter 10, page 74)

A Cash Flow Forecast clears your mind for productive thinking.

Warning: This is a tough section; take it slowly, a little at a time. Discuss it with others—but master it!

1. Why do a Cash Flow Forecast?

Putting a Cash Flow Forecast on paper will give you the following:

- A format for planning the effective use of cash
- A schedule of anticipated cash receipts
- A schedule of priorities for payment of accounts
- A measure of the significance of unexpected changes in circumstances, i.e. reduction in sale, strikes, tight money situations, etc.
- A list, on paper, of all bill paying details.
- An estimate of money you need to finance day-to-day operations, perhaps the most important aspect of a cash flow projection.
- An outline to show you and the lender that you will generate sufficient cash to make loan payments.

2. How Often?

Cash flow planning should be continuous since most lines of credit are renewed annually. Your forecast must be redone at least once a year, but preferably monthly, or quarterly.

Don't put the Cash Flow Forecast away and forget it. If you don't meet a sales objective or have a sudden unexpected payment to make, or some other contingency take out the Cash Flow and work through it again, whether it's review time or not. You will immediately see the effect of the change on your cash position and can illustrate any revised loan requirements to your lender.

Effective cash management is essential to survival and increased profits. Don't leave cash flow analysis to luck. You will lose.

The first step in preparing a Cash Flow Forecast is to estimate sales on a monthly basis. There are many yardsticks for estimating sales. A conservative forecast predicts financial results of bad times. An optimistic forecast will show the strain on working capital resulting from better than expected operations. A sales forecast in the middle should be the point around which plans are made.

Then, estimate what sales will be cash and what will be credit. If last year's sales were 10% cash and 90% credit and you do not change your credit policies, chances are the same will occur this year. If you sell on credit, take into account when you expect to collect accounts receivable, and be sure to allow for uncollectables.

The next step is to plan for accounts payable on a monthly basis according to your sales projections. For example, if you pay your invoices on a 30-day basis, then the cash expenditures for January's purchases will be made in February. If you can obtain trade credit for longer terms, then cash outlays can be delayed.

3. Cash Flow Worksheet

Now that cash collections and payments on purchases have been estimated, use a cash flow work sheet to list expected cash transactions for the month. Remember—Only list the actual cash you are expecting to receive or spend.

It is important that the Cash Flow Forecast is completed on an ongoing basis and revised as the situation changes. A computer-generated spreadsheet is useful for this purpose. After each month, put the actual cash flow figures next to the planned figures and compare them. If the planned figures vary considerably with the actual, it may be necessary to revise the figures for succeeding months. In extreme situations, it may be necessary to rethink the particular aspects of the business operation.

A Cash Flow Forecast assists in financial planning, inventory purchases and forming credit and collection policies. It also serves as an early indicator of when expenses are getting out of line. A typical format follows. This tool is fundamental and one of the most important for controlling the business.

Cash Flow Worksheet

Month ___________ Year _____________

a) Cash Receipts

1	Cash sales	________
2	Collection from Accounts Receivable	________
3	Term loan proceeds	________
4	Sale of fixed assets	________
5	Other cash received	________
6	TOTAL CASH IN	========

b) Cash Disbursements

7	Rent (include leases)	________
8	Management salaries	________
9	Other salaries and wages	________
10	Legal and Audit Fees	________
11	Utilities	________
12	Telephone	________
13	Repairs and maintenance	________
14	Licenses and municipal taxes	________
15	Insurance	________
16	Other operating expenses	________
17	Payments on Purchase of fixed assets	________
18	Interest on loans	________
19	Payments on Mortgages/Term loans	________
20	Income Tax Payments	________
21	Cash Dividends Paid	________
22	Payments on Accounts Payable	________
23	Other Cash Expenses	________
24	TOTAL CASH OUT	========

c) Reconciliation of Cash Flow

25	Opening Cash Balance	________
26	Add: Cash in (Line 6)	________
27	Deduct: Cash Out (Line 24)	________
28	Surplus (or deficit)	________
29	CLOSING CASH BALANCE	========

Choosing Child Care Facilities (chapter 11, page 76)

This is a checklist to help gather information about child care facilities. Make notes, you'll then have data for comparisons between various facilities.

- Does the center share your beliefs and values regarding childcare?
- Is the facility recommended by someone you trust?
- Is the facility licensed?
- Is it in a convenient area?
- Are hours of operation flexible and do they suit your schedule?
- Does it takes care of children in the same age group as yours?
- Does it have enough staff to give children proper care and attention?
- Is staff well-trained?
- Is staff turnover low?
- Are its fees competitive?
- Does it have a waiting list?
- Does it have space available right now?
- Have you met the caregiver and observed the facilities and programs?
- Is there a safe and exciting outdoor play area?
- Are there varied indoor play areas?
- Do music, dancing and open-ended art receive emphasis?

As in all else in this book, take your time, really do your homework.
Your peace of mind on this issue is vital.

Dealing With Stress (chapter 11, page 77)

To help you determine you status as a "Time Manager."

- Do you know your schedule for tomorrow? For next week?
- Do you know what you want to accomplish tomorrow? Next week?
- Does your schedule include time for important people in your life?
- Do you leave time between appointments to eat, prepare for the next meeting, relax or accommodate sudden changes?
- Do you know your high and low energy times?
- Do you set realistic deadlines for current projects?
- Do you break large or complex projects into manageable parts?
- Do you work with reliable people?
- Do you delegate tasks that can easily be handled by someone else?
- Does your schedule include time to think, create and plan?
- Can you say "no" without feeling anxious or guilty?

A Filing System That Will Work (chapter 12, page 84)

1. Administration
1-1 General Administration
1-2 Automobile
1-3 Courier Service
1-4 Depreciation
1-5 Equipment
1-6 Electrical
1-7 Furniture
1-8 Insurance
1-9 Licenses
1-10 Mail
1-11 Telephone
1-12 Utilities

2. Communications
2-1 General Communications
2-2 Advertising
2-3 Contacts
2-4 Brochures and Promotional Material
2-5 Government Correspondence
2-6 General Correspondence (if or when individual files are not opened)
2-7 Clippings, newspaper/magazine
2-8 Public Relations
2-9 Subscriptions
2-10 Competition

3. Consultants and Professionals
3-1 General Consultants and Professionals
3-2 Administration and Management (including office systems)
3-3 Business-specific
3-4 Computer
3-5 Financial
3-6 Marketing

4. Education and Training
4-1 General Education and Training
4-2 Client/Customer Education
4-3 Business Education and Training
4-5 Seminars and Workshops
4-6 Business Management Training Plan

5. Financial

5-1 General Financial
5-2 Accountants (and Auditor)
5-3 Accounts Payable
5-4 Accounts Receivable
5-6 Bank - Loans/Credit
5-7 Bank - Signing Authority
5-8 Bank - Statements
5-9 Bank - Reconciliation
5-10 Business Financing
5-11 Taxation
5-12 Contracts

6. Forms

6-1 General Forms
6-2 Alphabetical list by form to end of section

7. Legal

7-1 General Legal
7-2 Business Structure
7-3 Lawyer, Solicitor's Firm
7-4 Licensing Requirements
7-5 Municipal By-laws

8. Marketing

8-1 General Marketing
8-2 Contacts
8-3 Trade Association Information
8-4 Industry Events (trade fairs, shows, conferences, conventions)
8-5 Annual Events — local and regional
8-6 Customer Profile
8-7 Target Market Information
8-8 Marketing
8-9 Publicity and Promotion

9. Personnel

9-1 General Personnel
9-2 Applications (résumés)
9-3 Casual and Temporary Employment
9-4 Benefits
9-5 Deduction Information
9-6 Payroll Information
9-7 Taxation—Employee
9-8 Workers' Compensation

10. Products and Services

10-1 General Products and Services
10-2 alphabetical to end of section, products and services files

11. Clients' Files

11-1 General Clients
11-2 Leads and Prospective Clients
11-3 Individual client files, alphabetical by company or individual's name

12. Accounts Payable

12-1 General Accounts Payable (payment information)
12-2 Accounts Payable (bills paid)
12-3 Accounts Payable (alphabetical by supplier)

13. Accounts Receivable

13-1 General Accounts Receivable
13-2 Accounts Receivable (received)
13-3 Accounts Receivable (alphabetical by name of business or person)

Read Any Of These? (chapter 12, page 86)

The following is a list of instructive books that I have recently read. It is not intended to suggest an exhaustive list!

1. *The End of Work*, Jeremy Rivkin, Putnam, 1995
2. *In the Shelter of Each Other*, Mary Pipher, Ballantine, 1997
3. *Mompreneurs*, Ellen Parlapiano & Patricia Cobe, Perigee, 1996
4. *Ecoforestry: The Art and Science of Sustainable Forestry Use*, Drengson & Taylor, New Society, 1997
5. *Job Shift*, William Bridges, Addison-Wesley, 1996
6. *The E Myth Revisited*, Michael Gerber, Harper business, 1995
7. *Clicking*, Faith Popcorn, Harper Collins, 1996
8. *The Power of Superfoods*, Sam Graci, Prentice Hall, 1997
9. *Everybody's Food Safe Kitchen*, Sheri Nielsen, Everyone's Kitchen Ventures, 1996
10. *Sacred Moments*, Linda Kavelin Popov, Penguin, 1996
11. *The New Nutrition*, and, *Hormonal Health*, Michael Colgan, Apple Publishing, 1995, 1996
12. *The Heat is On: The High Stakes Battle over Earth's Threatened Climate*, Ross Goldspan, Addison-Wesley, 1998
13. *I've Been Rich, I've Been Poor. Rich is Better*, Judy Resnick, Golden Books, New York, 1998
14. *To Taunt a Wounded Tiger*, Tony Bruce, Glendambo Publishing, 1997
15. *Stopping—How to be Still*, David Kundtz, Canari Press, 1998
16. *Taking Care of Business*, Heather Robertson, Fenn, 1997
17. *Work Less Live More*, Paula Brook, Doubleday Canada, 1997
18. *Business Capital for Women*, Card & Miller, MacMillan, 1996
19. *The Female Advantage: Women's Ways of Leadership*, Helgesen, Currency Doubleday, 1990
20. *Tax Shift*, Alan Durning, Northwest Environment Watch, Seattle, 1998

> *Look after your body — Where else are you going to live?*
>
> – Unknown

Primary Research Techniques (chapter 14, page 100)

	PROS	CONS
Questionnaires, mailed or handed out	♦ Consistent and objective ♦ Can calculate responses ♦ Additional questionnaires can be prepared if necessary	♦ Inflexible ♦ Time consuming to prepare, print and calculate responses ♦ Need many answers for statistically reliable conclusions
Surveys prepared by college/business students	♦ Inexpensive ♦ Third party survey prepared under guidance of program information instructor ♦ Many students can carry out a range of data collection ♦ Good facilities for reporting	♦ Priorities and time frame may not be the same as yours ♦ Inexperience at getting information
Informal talks with Customers	♦ Open and revealing responses ♦ Inexpensive ♦ Opportunity to ask unprepared questions ♦ Can/should be carried on continuously	♦ Must prepare key issues in advance ♦ Responses may be vague, contradictory, without thought ♦ Must gather many responses for statistically reliable conclusions
Interviews (one on one)	♦ Face to face discussions ♦ Combines objective with open-ended, subjective information ♦ Opportunity to obtain additional comments ♦ Often professionals planning, thus increasing reliability	♦ Requires more prep time to develop closed and (probing) questions ♦ Time consuming to arrange appointments ♦ Few people willing to be interviewed ♦ Costly

	PROS	CONS
Focus Groups (8 - 12 people)	♦ In-depth probing ♦ Wide open responses ♦ Observation of interaction, dynamics of participants ♦ Great for forming "theses," for broader statistical validation	♦ Requires costly professional facilitators ♦ Additional cost of room and observers ♦ Often a preliminary, requiring follow-up studies
Suppliers, distributors	♦ Inside knowledge of industry ♦ Knowledge of players, trends and quirks	♦ Could favor existing dealers ♦ Jaded comments with narrow viewpoint
Competitors	♦ Observe traffic counts, average sale checks and customer patterns ♦ Observations on any market aspect i.e., location, advertising, pricing, etc. ♦ Competition in other communities often willing to talk to someone who won't be a threat	♦ Biased ♦ Unwilling to talk to potential competitor ♦ Travel and long distance costs
Retired from the Industry	♦ No axe to grind ♦ Objective and open ♦ Knowledge of industry, its pitfalls and who is succeeding ♦ Possible mentor, advisor	♦ Information may be dated ♦ Jaded and tired of business concerns
Mentor	♦ Objective ♦ Can analyze situation and be brutally frank ♦ Can assess your own capacity, resources and managerial ability ♦ Can advise on strategy and major decisions	♦ May lack specific industry knowledge ♦ Not always available on a no fee basis

Questions to Help With Trade Show Planning (chapter 15, page 107)

- Is it a wholesale or retail audience?
- What volume of visitors is expected?
- What handouts will you need: business cards, brochures, price lists, publicity articles?
- What products and how many of each will you need for sale? A range of products and prices should be represented.
- Is the entry fee a set amount or a percentage of sales or both? Include in your budget.
- What is the show theme; can you tie into it?
- Who pays for signage at the booth? Is it keyed to certain colors or graphics?
- How should you staff? Be realistic. Exhibit work is taxing, both mentally and physically. Staff should not be on duty without a break for more than three or four hours.
- What educational events do you want you or your staff to attend?
- What demonstrations can you mount? What props and expertise do you need for the expected booth?
- What designated services in the Exhibitor's Kit are you required to use?
- Does this show make awards? Winning in any category can be used as part of your promotion and publicity during the next year.

If you are exhibiting outside your territory, familiarize yourself with local rules:

- Do you need a license?
- How are you required to report sales tax?
- Are there product and labeling restrictions?
- Do you need extra insurance coverage?

Are there locations which would be preferable for your booth? (Near the refreshment stands is guaranteed to be among the heaviest traffic areas!) A request for a favored location may mean a higher rental fee or an early reservation, probably both.

Trade Show Budget Items (chapter 15, page 108)

- booth rental
- display booth structure (either to rent or build)
- signage
- transportation (both ways)
- insurance during transit
- display booth
- signage
- demonstration products
- promotional materials
- services at the site
- booth set-up
- electrical connection
- lighting, curtains, carpets
- optional services
- business promotion
- notices/invitations to customers and contacts
- brochures, business cards
- advertising, publicity
- giveaways, prize promotions
- demonstration materials
- personal expenses (all staff)
- food
- lodging
- travel
- shoplifting (allow 10% for losses at a retail exhibit, 5% at wholesale)
- unforeseen expenses (add 10%)

About the Author

David Bryn-Jones graduated from the Harvard Business School and has considerable writing and research experience in both the US and Canada.

Following several years in Brand Management work at Procter & Gamble (Canada), Bryn-Jones then spent some fifteen years in senior account management positions with advertising agencies in New York, Montreal, Toronto, Vancouver and Chicago.

During this period, Bryn Enterprises Limited was formed to develop drive-in restaurants, financed by selling equity to friends and associates, and securing small business government financial assistance. This business was sold after seven restaurants were developed in order that Bryn-Jones and family could return to the sea of their beloved West Coast.

Following a series of entrepreneurial endeavors, primarily in real estate sales and property development, Bryn-Jones concluded his active business career by serving as the Executive Director of a major non-profit women's medical society.

Now retired to Salt Spring Island, one of the beautiful and peaceful islands in the Gulf of Georgia separating Washington State from British Columbia, Bryn-Jones is promoting his theme that "Women Make Great Entrepreneurs"— and that the planet needs them.

Success

TO
LAUGH
OFTEN and love much;

to win the respect of intelligent people and the affection of children; to earn the approbation of honest critics and endure the betrayal of false friends; to appreciate beauty; to find the best in others; to give one's self; to leave the world a bit better, whether by a healthy child, a garden patch, or redeemed social condition; to have played and laughed with enthusiasm and sung with exultation; to know even one life has breathed easier because you have lived —

THIS
IS
TO
HAVE
SUCCEEDED.

– Ralph Waldo Emerson

Inspiring Women Entrepreneur Organizations

The principals or key people involved with the companies listed alphabetically below have all provided me with material from which I have developed the wonderful real-life role model women entrepreneur stories from all over North America so vital to this book.

There is great diversity in the stories of these 49 companies, interspersed in chapters throughout the book (see *Contents*). From mighty to modest, struggling to established, each story reveals some imprint of that woman entrepreneur's courage, convictions and drive.

It is fun to note that, in many cases, these entrepreneurs are succeeding with a shoot-from-the hip, go-for-it style… quite different from the step-by-step, well researched, business plan approach I recommend. I honor these entrepreneurs. It just proves, there is always more than one way. More power to them. They have **done** it and that is the real point.

Company	**Location**	**page**
African Communications Group	Cambridge, MA	30
American Tours International Inc.	Los Angeles, CA	26
Artist	Old Chelsea, PQ	142
Barb's Buns	Salt Spring Island, BC	130
Big Printing Inc.	Brea, CA	140
Boardwalk Greens	Salt Spring Island, BC	34
Bureau 2000 International Inc.	Malibu, CA	139
Carpe Diem Coffee Roasting Company	North Berwick, ME	97
Cat's Meow Creations	Victoria, BC	138
Chefwear Inc.	Chicago, IL	131
Congdon's Aids to Daily Living	Edmonton, AB	134
Dabney, Resnick, Imperial	Los Angeles, CA	33
Encore Seniors Education Centre	Cornwall, ON	137
Evelyn's Wig & Breast Prosthetic Service	Lorette, MB	129
Everlasting Summer	Salt Spring Island, BC	67
Focus On Caring	Calgary, AB	135
French Rags	Los Angeles, CA	28
Friends of the Family	Toronto, ON	72
Gaynor Minden Inc.	New York, NY	68

These women entrepreneurs have adopted Emile Zola's philosophy:
"I've come to live out loud."